YORK CITY

— FIGHTING BACK —

DAVE FLETT

AMBERLEY

ACKNOWLEDGEMENTS

Many thanks to my past and present sports desk colleagues Steve Carroll, Claire Hughes, Martin Jarred, Tony Kelly, Stuart Martel, Peter Martini, Hugh McDougall and Dave Stanford. Thanks also to my wife, Nikki, and our children, Matthew, Thomas and Ruby.

To York City's No. 1 fan, Kath Rowe, and my Nan, Connie Featherstone, a voracious reader of books. Both were with us at the start of this project, but had sadly passed away by its end.

1

'LIKE A STRIPPER'S KNICKERS'

'We'll be Back' declared one banner as York City's decaying Bootham Crescent ground bid farewell to the Football League in May 2004. Quite when the relegated Minstermen – League members for seventy-five consecutive years – would return remained unspecified, however.

Terry Doyle – the club's finance director at the time – was braver when, weeks later, he insisted that York's aim must be to become the 'Arsenal of the Conference' during the new season. The Gunners had just completed a historic unbeaten campaign on their way to the Premier League title. Sadly, for Doyle and City's long-suffering supporters, any resemblance their team bore to Arsène Wenger's Invincibles during 2004/05 was confined to their new white-sleeved red tops.

Promotion back to the League, it soon became clear, was going to be no quick fix for this proud club who, just nine years earlier, had won 3-0 at Old Trafford against a Manchester United team featuring the likes of David Beckham and Ryan Giggs. A 3-1 defeat by old Yorkshire foes Doncaster, coupled with victories for relegation rivals Scunthorpe and Rochdale, had confirmed that the Minstermen would spend 2004/05 – the season that marked the golden anniversary of the club's famous FA Cup semi-final appearance – as a non-League outfit.

The Doncaster game was the eighteenth of a twenty-match, season-ending sequence without a win, which set an unwanted club record. Incredibly, the same York side had also taken their place in the history books at the start of the campaign by winning their first four League contests. In fact, the Minstermen had only slipped into the bottom half of the table for the first time on 21 February, but were relegated little more than two months later. The famous walled city had been home to a professional team plying its trade in one of the top four divisions of this country, albeit never the first and only briefly the second, since 1929 – a year when BBC transmitters were used to broadcast the first television programmes on John Logie Baird's experimental sets. Few alive, therefore, could remember watching their football under the auspices of any other body.

Having seen their Football League fate sealed at Doncaster, however, York's final home game of the 2003/04 season against Leyton Orient saw supporters invade the pitch – surprisingly, not in anger. Instead, they chose to express their continued support for rookie manager Chris Brass and the club, if not some of its players. Many fans were grateful to still have a team to follow, with the Supporters' Trust having rescued the club from certain closure the previous season by raising the money needed to bring it out of administration, following the damaging reigns of previous owners Douglas Craig and John Batchelor.

The spectre of Craig, indeed, still hung over the club in 2004. Having persuaded Batchelor, his successor at the Bootham Crescent helm, to tear up the club's lease on the ground, Craig was threatening to evict the team from their traditional home at the time. During his tenure as chairman, the fierce Scotsman had transferred ownership of the stadium and training ground from the club into a holding company. He was a director of the company – Bootham Crescent Holdings – along with fellow former City boardroom members Barry Swallow and Colin Webb. As Brass's men slipped out of the League, Craig was demanding a sizeable seven-figure sum to sell the assets back to the club. Swallow's role in the whole episode was particularly painful, given his status as a playing legend for York – one that would be subsequently tarnished forever.

Having assumed control of the club, the Trust appointed a board of directors who, at the start of the 2003/04 campaigns, had decided to replace Terry Dolan with former Burnley defender Brass as manager. Club captain Brass was only twenty-seven at the time, but had impressed everybody with his maturity and commitment to the club during its darkest days. Unsurprisingly, having taken the club down to the Conference, he was both emotional and amazed by the supporters' response at the end of that Orient game and said, 'We should have had tomatoes thrown at us and been spat at but that's not testimony to myself, it's testimony to the fans at this football club. They are intelligent.

'Events in the past are not being used as excuses but they certainly have not helped the cause. I hope the players have also realised what the club means to the fans because they will get an even better reception when they actually win something.'

The team had set another club record during the 2003/04 campaign by hitting the target just thirty-five times in forty-six games. Young defender Chris Smith, twenty-two, was among those players subsequently released before a team, including six teenagers in the starting line-up, helped the club at least exit the League with dignity, following a 0-0 draw at Swansea – who could not have foreseen their climb up to English football's premier division seven years later. Brass, having signed a three-and-a-half-year contract as manager midway through the season and prior to the slump, at least had three months to build a team good enough to reclaim the club's League status, rather than the three weeks he had been afforded to assemble a squad a year earlier when taking over from Dolan. He opted for experience, recruiting seasoned thirty-something campaigners Steve Davis, Kevin Donovan, Paul Crichton, Shaun Smith and Paul Groves. Andy Bishop was also signed after turning down a new contract from then Walsall manager Paul Merson, and fellow forward Paul Robinson – once famously preferred to Alan Shearer by Ruud Gullit in a Newcastle *v.* Sunderland derby clash – was brought in to improve City's fortunes in front of goal too. Other additions included midfielder Gary Pearson and centre-back Chris Clarke.

While Groves and Donovan were clearly past their best, they would show commitment throughout the season, and Bishop offered glimpses of promise as well, but the other signings would prove poor acquisitions. Clarke only lasted five mistake-riddled games and Crichton, an understudy to Norwich 'keeper Robert Green the previous season, left the club after arguing with City supporters during a 4-0 defeat at Gravesend & Northfleet. Davis and Pearson were crocked for the majority of the season, while Smith looked a shadow of the distinguished left-back he was at Crewe and spent long spells out of favour. Perhaps most disappointingly, given he once moved from Newcastle to Wimbledon for £1.5 million, Robinson contributed just two goals all season.

Off the pitch, City were at least given a boost before the start of the new season when they secured a £2-million loan from the Football Stadia Improvement Fund. The money would be used to pay Craig, Swallow and Webb their ransom money, putting the club back in control of its own destiny. But six-figure annual loan repayments would need to be met after Craig received a sum of £1,084,000, while Swallow and Webb each pocketed £172,661 – receiving eleven times the price of the shares they had bought for £1 apiece. A profit of £83,000 for the year ending 30 June 2004 was also announced by the club – representing a transformation from the twelve-week operating loss of £332,338 that had been racked up honouring existing contracts a year ago during the first three months of the Trust's ownership.

Brass was optimistic at the start of the new campaign, although his team were not among the bookmakers' favourites for promotion. 'There's always a surprise package and it might be ourselves because not many people seem to fancy us,' Brass reasoned. 'I will be disappointed if we don't mount some sort of challenge and that means looking at the play-offs.' But, ahead of the first game of the season at Aldershot, former City defender Ray Warburton, who lined up against his old club, ominously warned the Conference new boys, 'I think York will find out that the Conference is a hard league … You don't go down and just win every game.' Shots skipper Warburton went on to lead the previous season's beaten play-off finalists to a 2-0 win, during which City debutant Pearson was sent off for an alleged headbutt.

Clarke was also given a torrid time by impressive Shots strikers Aaron McLean and Roscoe D'Sane, while Jon Challinor scored the first goal against City in the Conference midway through the second half, just two minutes after coming on as a substitute. There was cause for some celebration, however, when York ended a seven-month wait for a win in their next match, overcoming part-time Tamworth 2-0 with Groves and Robinson on target. A 3-0 home humbling against Hereford, including blunders from Smith and Crichton, then gave City a stern reality check, with the team booed off the pitch.

A board meeting was subsequently held, informing Brass of a specific deadline to turn the team's fortunes around. Managing director Jason McGill added, 'This is Chris's team so we have got to give him a chance but, like anything, that goes so far.' A 4-0 defeat at Gravesend and Northfleet heaped further pressure on Brass, with 'keeper Crichton's week-to-week contract terminated after allegations, which he later refuted, that he hurled abuse back at disgruntled supporters. Feelings ran so high at half-time in the game that a steward had to retrieve Crichton's glove bag from the back of the net in front of baying City fans.

The part-time Gravesend team included a farmer, a stockbroker, a plumber, a teacher and a shop floor manager from Next, while first-choice striker Roy Essandoh even missed the start of the game after getting stuck in traffic on the M11.

City's 'keeper woes intensified in the next match when Chris Porter was harshly sent off twenty minutes into a 1-0 home defeat to Accrington Stanley. David Stockdale, later to graduate to Premier League stardom and full England squads, was given his home debut as a consequence at the age of eighteen, and responded well with a man-of-the-match performance. For once, the supporters' ire was directed at the officials rather than their team.

City went on to score three goals for the first time in fifty games under Brass and enjoyed their first away win in nine months after defeating Dagenham & Redbridge 3-0. Darren Dunning (two) and Groves were on target. But, following a 1-0 defeat at Crawley, Viv Busby was brought back to the club to help Brass and his assistant Lee Nogan with coaching. Busby is held in high esteem at Bootham Crescent, having been Denis Smith's No. 2 when York became the first team to win more than 100 points in a season on their way to the 1984 old fourth-division title.

Welcoming his arrival at the time, Brass said, 'This is an exciting appointment as Viv has a great reputation and a successful track record. He has a vast knowledge of coaching techniques and great motivational skills which can only benefit the team.' Busby, meanwhile, immediately made it clear that he was not interested in succeeding Brass as manager. 'I'm not here to upset any apple-carts or take anybody's job,' he insisted. 'I'm just hoping I can bring a bit of experience to go alongside their youth.' Former Newcastle striker Busby watched on as City drew 0-0 with Northwich – the sixth game in which the team had failed to score during their opening eight Conference matches.

The first calls of 'Brass Out' were heard at Bootham Crescent following the final whistle and, in the next home match, fifteen Leigh RMI fans turned up to see their side win only their second away point from a possible forty-two during a 1-1 draw. City's goal came courtesy of a Dunning penalty.

Some hope was offered when Bishop opened his City account in his tenth outing during a 2-0 win at Burton, and the Minstermen climbed into thirteenth place after a 3-1 home victory over Stevenage. Cries of 'We Love You City, We Do' rang out from the David Longhurst Stand during that match, and the players even received a standing ovation at half-time from their success-starved supporters. But the team were given a 4-0 hiding at table-topping Barnet in mid-October, and a board statement issued afterwards pointed out that 'playing performances are under constant review'.

A 3-1 fourth qualifying round FA Cup exit followed at Carlisle and, afterwards, 88 per cent of respondents to an unofficial website internet poll suggested it was time for Brass to be relieved of his duties. They got their wish after a 3-1 home defeat to fellow strugglers Forest Green when visiting striker Charlie Griffin scored a hat-trick.

It was a sad, if inevitable, end to Brass's reign, as he was booed every time he touched the ball towards the end of the game. Home fans even resorted to cheering on the visitors, while slow handclapping their own players. Commenting on his treatment afterwards, Brass said, 'The flak is not nice and I asked the players how they would feel if they had to take it. I fight tooth and nail for them and take a lot of crap, but there comes a time when you have to get a bit back.' His team had taken sixteen points from sixteen games in the Conference but Brass stayed on as a player, due to the terms of his three-and-a-half year contract. Jason McGill revealed the decision was unanimous among the club's directors and Busby was placed in temporary charge but immediately admitted that 'it was a very difficult decision' for him to take over from Brass. 'It was a massive bombshell and my first reaction was to say that both Lee and I should also go,' he revealed. 'Chris said I should take on the job, adding that he would carry on as a player and would do his best for us. Chris has been outstanding in a time that is absolutely gutting for him. In a way nothing much has changed. The three of us will still be in it together and give it a go. I have not even thought about whether I would want the job permanently. I don't believe in titles and I've told the players I don't want to be called gaffer or boss.'

Busby added that he felt the team could still mount a promotion challenge, saying, 'It is still not too late to get out of the division. You only need to put a run of five or six wins in a ten-match spell together.' Dunning, meanwhile, admitted that the players needed to take responsibility for the manager's dismissal, adding, 'As a manager, I think Chris did everything he possibly could. He was one of the best man-managers I have ever come across. But when you cross that whitewash it has got to be down to the players to do the business and for whatever reason we have not.' Brass later confessed, 'I wasn't surprised by the decision but I was gutted and I told the board that. I said the situation had arisen not for the want of trying and I had wanted to make things a success but the board have these decisions to make and we have now moved on. As a team, we all wanted success but unfortunately it did not happen and I want to say sorry to the fans that I could not deliver it. All I'm concentrating on now is using all my energy as a player to get results for York City and the new manager.'

As Busby suggested, though, striker Bishop soon confirmed that few things had changed under the caretaker boss. 'Viv and Chris Brass have exactly the same ideas and we have been doing exactly the same things in training,' he pointed out. Busby's first decision as manager also saw him hand the captaincy back to Brass, with the armband having been inherited by Dunning during Davis's injury absence. In Busby's first game in charge, City went down 1-0 at Woking but the temporary manager, who was working without a contract, felt the team deserved at least a point, saying, 'If we keep working like that week in, week out, we will get results.' Despite the reaction during his last game in charge, Brass remained popular within circles of the City faithful with a banner at Woking proclaiming 'Chris Brass is Our Number One'. On seeing it, Busby added, 'That was terrific.'

The former Sunderland coach even suggested the club were wrong to dismiss Brass as manager, saying, 'For me, the board reacted to the pressure of the crowd at the Forest Green match and it was not the right decision.' City then sprung a surprise by beating high-flying Carlisle 2-1, heralding talk afterwards that the match might have just marked the birth of Busby's Babes, with seven home players aged nineteen or under by the final whistle at Bootham Crescent. Kane Ashcroft, Michael Staley and Lee Grant were all given their full home debuts and were joined by fellow under-twenties Stockdale and Sean Davies in the starting line-up. Lev Yalcin and Graeme Law were also introduced from the bench.

Peter Murphy's twentieth-minute dismissal had assisted the youngsters, however, and the optimism proved short-lived as Northwich inflicted a demoralising 3-0 defeat on the Minstermen. After that match, Dunning admitted, 'We are in a dogfight now. They were not a better team than us but we went down like the *Titanic*.' A little light relief was provided soon after with the signing of a second Paul Robinson from Tranmere. To differentiate between the two, his namesake became Paul D. Robinson. Sadly, the 'D' did not stand for deadly or dynamic – but Derrick!

The woe continued when the Minstermen were thrashed 5-1 at Scarborough on Boxing Day – a result that represented a heaviest-ever defeat to their North Yorkshire rivals. Horrendous mistakes by Grant, Brass and Smith, who was also sent off, contributed to the visitors' downfall. Busby vainly tried to point to positives afterwards, saying, 'Let's see if we can eliminate these mistakes and take away the positives because we passed the ball well, created some chances and scored a goal.' The experienced Groves was more forthright in his assessment. 'Our backsides were tanned,' he admitted. Rookie 'keeper Stockdale was taken out of the firing line for the next match – a 2-1 home defeat to Burton when Brass also suffered season-ending, cruciate knee ligament damage.

A truly *annus horribilis*, 2004, had ended with just thirty-one points taken in twelve months, with loud choruses of 'You're Not Fit to Wear the Shirt' emanating from an angry David Longhurst Stand. Then, 2005 did not get off to the best of starts either, when Scarborough completed the double over the Minstermen with a 2-0 victory at Bootham Crescent that left the team just one place and two points above the relegation zone. Scarborough's goals came in the eighty-ninth minute and stoppage time through strikers Chris Senior and Tony Hackworth. Communications director Sophie McGill admitted afterwards that the board had now readdressed their priorities for the season. 'I really would have to say it is about consolidation and avoiding relegation now,' she stressed.

Busby finally managed to win an away point during a 2-2 draw at play-off hopefuls Stevenage, where on-loan Doncaster defender Jon Maloney and seventeen-year-old midfielder Byron Webster found the net. The temporary chief then offered to quit, however, following a 3-0 FA Trophy defeat at Burton soon afterwards. 'The performances are like a stripper's knickers – they are up one week and down the next,' he complained. 'All the players have to do is give their all for the club for ninety minutes on a Saturday but, if they aren't going to do it for me, then I will have to talk to the board and offer to step aside and let somebody else have a go. I've done as much as I can but if they want me to stay I will do and will keep working at it.'

Following Busby's outburst, it was announced that Bootham Crescent would be called KitKat Crescent for two years after an £100,000 sponsorship agreement with Nestlé Rowntree. The money was subsequently used to complete the £2.1-million deal to buy back the club's stadium and training facilities from Bootham Crescent Holdings. Commenting on the name change, Jason McGill said, 'KitKat Crescent was the obvious choice of name for the ground as the product is manufactured in York and, like KitKat, City's home strip is red-and-white. We felt it was important to maintain the word Crescent, instead of Stadium or Park, and hope our supporters are pleased with the name and are proud the club is associated with such a prestigious brand.'

Unsurprisingly, not everybody was in favour of the decision, with club historian Dave Batters saying, 'My initial reaction to KitKat Crescent is "dear me" and I don't like it.

'To me, Bootham Crescent will always be Bootham Crescent. The name is steeped in seventy or eighty years of history and has a nice ring to it. I feel a lot of sadness about the name change, but it's a sign of the times I suppose. Yorkie Crescent would not have been brilliant but it would have been better.'

The Sun national newspaper delighted in the new name, however, even naming a chocolate footballing XI, with manager Keith Curle-y Wurly in charge of the likes of Hernan Toffee Crespo, Robbie Flake and Gary Revel.

City went on to enjoy a couple of breaks in the first match at their newly monikered home when they defeated Morecambe 1-0 after a dubiously awarded penalty converted by Bishop. The visitors also rattled the crossbar twice. Despite the club's travails, Richard Harris – a former factory worker at Nestlé's chocolate rivals Terry's – then chose to blow nearly all his redundancy money on a ten-year season ticket. 'Well, it can't get any worse,' he reasoned.

Following a 2-0 home defeat to Aldershot, in an attempt to improve matters City's board replaced Busby with former Rotherham and Sheffield United manager Billy McEwan. Nogan, assistant to both Brass and Busby, also departed, which left McEwan, fresh from nine years in various different coaching roles at Derby, to work without a No. 2 for the rest of the season. Ambitious from the start, McEwan said on his appointment, 'We might need a bit of patience and perseverance but we want to try and be the best in the Conference.

'I don't know how long that will take but, when the players go on the pitch, they will represent me and you (the supporters) and they will have pride in wearing the badge. I want Conference Manager of the Month awards and to be successful. I have not come here to mess about and pick my money up. I have come to do my job which is to help get York City back in the League.'

Outlining his expectations of the players, McEwan added, 'My teams have to be organised, disciplined and fit.' On the new manager, Jason McGill predicted, 'I feel Billy will turn things around in terms of discipline, coaching, tactics and organisation.' Disgraced former chairman Craig also admitted that he felt McEwan was a good candidate when he was interviewed for the job back in 1991 before John Ward was appointed, but added that he 'had a reputation for being a bit wild which I suspect he still has'.

Busby departed, accusing the board of going behind his back after learning of interviews for the manager's job following a phone call from a player. However, McEwan, who counts Alex Ferguson and Kenny Dalglish as close friends and played for Brighton under Brian Clough, wasted no time in putting his own stamp on the club. He cleaned the toilets himself during his first week in the job after being disgusted by their condition, and switched the dugouts so the home bench was closer to the David Longhurst Stand. 'I felt it would benefit the bench to be closer to the York fans on the terrace,' he explained. 'We need lots of vocal support over the coming weeks.'

The Minstermen earned a 1-1 draw at Forest Green in McEwan's first game in charge, with Bishop's penalty cancelled out by a harshly awarded spot-kick against Groves. The new boss was relatively pleased, saying, 'I thought we played very well considering all the turmoil that has been going on at the club over the last week.' Better followed when, despite making the 300-mile journey on the day of the match due to financial constraints, the Minstermen fielded a new 4-5-1 formation to spring a big surprise by winning 1-0 at play-off hopefuls Exeter. Dave Merris got the only goal of the game – one of the visitors' two shots on the night compared to Exeter's eighteen. Recalled right-back Law, meanwhile, gave an insight into disciplinarian McEwan's managerial style afterwards, revealing that all the players had been issued with a two-page document about standards on and off the pitch. 'It was about rules and what he expects of us,' Law said. 'We are being made to work hard and he's getting us organised.'

McEwan then presided over City's first back-to-back wins in fourteen months with a shock 2-1 home win over Barnet, courtesy of goals from Donovan and Maloney. 'We are a sick patient but getting better,' the new chief declared afterwards. But that patient took another turn for the worse, as the team failed to win any of their next nine games before a final-day triumph over Farnborough. A 1-0 defeat at Tamworth, where the visitors failed to muster a single shot on target, prompted McEwan to comment, 'It's like turning the QE2 around in the Atlantic. It will take time for us to start moving in the right direction.' McEwan also called on fans and local businesses to raise the £10,000 needed to continue running a reserve team in the following season's Pontins League with twenty donations of £500 each.

'At the moment, I have one arm tied behind my back and, if we get rid of the reserves, I will have two,' he argued. 'There's money in York. I can see that just by looking around.' The people of York responded to McEwan's request and raised the required amount in just twenty days. A delighted McEwan hailed 'a tremendous effort'.

Centre-back Maloney returned to Doncaster at the end of his three-month loan spell, having netted in his final match, a 2-2 draw at play-off hopefuls Accrington Stanley. The goal was his fourth for City, making him the team's second-top scorer behind Bishop. Due to favourable results elsewhere, safety was eventually secured in the most inglorious fashion ever following a 6-0 thumping at Carlisle. An exasperated McEwan admitted that he might walk away from the club at the end of the season afterwards when he said:

> I was brought in to save York City from dropping out of the Conference. That mission has been accomplished and, if I have to walk away at the end of the season, I can sleep knowing that I got nine points and two big wins to do that.
>
> I have to look at my own future and career now and will have to sit down with my wife and ask her if I need this. I will also be discussing with the board where we want to go but I am not going to kill myself put it that way.
>
> It's a massive, massive job and it would be the easiest thing to walk away but I will fight and scrap until the end of the season and then we will see where we go. The result shows how far the club has fallen and how big a mountain it has to climb.
>
> Nothing will be achieved here in one or two years. It's going to be a long-term job. The club hasn't got two bob so what can you do? I'm Billy McEwan not Billy Graham. I'm not a miracle worker.
>
> The match was absolutely embarrassing for York City Football Club. You would not see some of those things on a Sunday morning football pitch. I didn't say one word to the players after the game because I was absolutely disgusted with them. I feel sorry for the fans, not them. They have got to show how tough they are and what they are made of. If they don't then they can clear off because I am not interested in them.

Jason McGill, though, urged McEwan to stay, adding, 'Billy McEwan is undoubtedly the right person to take this club forward and turn around playing performances. He has achieved the aim of security this season and the board sincerely hopes he will continue his good work at York City.' A 4-0 defeat at Canvey Island followed, though, which left McEwan fuming again: 'Some of the defending was amateur and dire. It made me wonder why I have come back into management, but I have done. I must be off my head to put myself through it again but it's what I want to do. I want to get things right at this club although it's a massive, massive challenge.'

City ended a sorry campaign with their biggest home victory for more than ten years, beating Farnborough 4-0, but McEwan was in no mood for celebrations at the final whistle. Addressing supporters, who had spilled on to the pitch following the game, McEwan said, 'I have told the players it is not acceptable to celebrate now, or wait until the end of the season to win 4-0, because this club has got to be battling at the top end of the table and not the bottom.' York ended the campaign sixth from bottom without completing a league double against any of their rivals.

McEwan, subsequently, offered only three out-of-contract players – Dave Merris, Lev Yalcin and Graeme Law – new deals. Brass, meanwhile, remained under contract for a further two years and, on that problematic matter, McEwan said, 'He has declined two financial settlements in January and February and he's a big earner – far too big for this football club and astronomical for this level. I don't know how we will pay him over the summer with no money coming in.'

Above: Player-manager Chris Brass challenges for possession as Dave Merris and Chris Smith look on during the match that saw York City's relegation from the Football League confirmed at Doncaster in 2004. (David Harrison)

Left: Chris Brass trudges off Doncaster's Belle Vue pitch after relegation from the Football League is confirmed. (David Harrison)

York City supporters signal their intention for a swift return to the Football League during the final home game of the 2003/04 season against Leyton Orient. (Steve Bradshaw)

Chris Brass (second right) parades 2004 summer signings (from left to right) Paul D. Robinson, Steve Davis, and Paul Groves. (*The Press*, York)

Left: A sign of the times as Brass suffers his final defeat as manager at home to Forest Green. (*The Press* staff photographer)

Below: Viv Busby returns to Bootham Crescent, initially as Chris Brass' assistant before becoming caretaker manager. (Garry Atkinson)

2

'ACCRINGTON HAVE GOT MONEY, WE'VE GOT KITKATS'

Having inherited a 'Dad's Army' of ageing footballers on his arrival at Bootham Crescent, Billy McEwan decided there would only be room for one father figure at the club during 2005/06. In his new paternal role, McEwan made vibrancy a key quality during a summer recruitment drive that resulted in him fielding nobody in his team over the age of thirty all season Following the hip problem that restricted him to just fourteen starts for the club, Steve Davis reached a financial settlement over the remaining year left on his contract and promptly retired from the game at the age of thirty-six. Despite being under contract, Paul D. Robinson was told to find alternative employers and Chris Brass was neither included in the pre-season photo call, nor issued with a squad number, despite still having two years of his playing contract to run. 'It's nothing personal,' McEwan explained about the former manager. 'If he was the best player at the club, it's not the point. We just can't afford his wages.' Brass later joined Harrogate Town on loan.

Managing director Jason McGill, meanwhile, admitted the rookie board made a mistake in appointing Brass, saying, 'It was our decision and we have learnt from that. We have got somebody in now with experience and a football-managing pedigree. I think we will see a team that plays with heart, passion and pride because they will respect the manager.' McEwan returned for pre-season training with just three professionals to work with in Andy Bishop, Darren Dunning and Chris Porter. David Stockdale and Bryan Stewart later signed professional contracts, while Graeme Law, Lev Yalcin and Dave Merris also agreed new terms. The rest of the previous season's squad were shown the door, with McEwan announcing, 'We had a lot of old players last season and I think younger players need bringing in. We did have young players last season but they were just babies, and our older players were getting too old. I am committed to help the club grow again even if it will take a while. I want to play an important part in York City's resurgence and, with hard work, professionalism and the right players, I know we will all see better times at the club.'

Meanwhile, Leeds United youth academy coach Colin Walker was appointed as McEwan's assistant, and Scarborough centre-back Mark Hotte became the club's first summer signing. Released Hull City striker Clayton Donaldson was next in, with McEwan saying, 'He has a bit of pace and penetration. He's a young player who is very hungry for this chance.' Midfielder Mark Convery also signed. Centre-back Greg Heald followed, but then changed his mind, leaving McEwan to fume: 'He's wasted my time really. When things like that happen I think that players should be fined. The lad says that he's not got another club but he must think we are stupid in this neck of the woods to believe that.'

Nobody was immune from the ire of City's fiery Scot, as he proved when a fan heckled the team after they conceded the first goal in a 4-0 pre-season home defeat to Hartlepool. The City boss demanded he 'shut up and offer encouragement'. He later added, 'If fans are going to do that, then I won't be here. I am not having that, no way. I don't want those people back at KitKat Crescent. They are no good at York City. If they are not going to encourage young players who are trying to make their way in the game, then my message would be please keep away. Next year I will not play any public games in pre-season if that's the way we are going to have it. The majority of fans understand our problems but the other lot can stay away.'

Outlining an off-the-pitch problem, the club announced losses of £83,568 for the first Conference campaign. Trialists Nathan Peat, Joe O'Neill, Ashley Winn, Jamie Price, Emmanuel Panther, James Dudgeon, Ryan Mallon and Dave Pounder, meanwhile, all joined the club on a permanent basis during pre-season, and Darren Mansaran arrived on loan from Halifax. After Heald's U-turn and eventual move to Aldershot via a short spell with Burton, David McGurk returned to Bootham Crescent for his second loan spell with the club from Darlington – this time being signed up for six months. The club also reached a financial settlement with Robinson over the remaining year of his contract. After an unsuccessful spell with Aberdeen, the striker, still only twenty-six, admitted he was ready to turn his back on football. 'I'm a bit disillusioned and I might not play again,' he said. 'I will go out to work if I have to.' He never played full-time football again.

Fans bought into McEwan's vision for a new era at the club prior to the start of the campaign, as tam-o'-shanters and Billy Mac's Barmy Army t-shirts sold well in the club shop. But the manager refused to comment on his side's potential before the new campaign, saying, 'The team have never played together and you can't assemble a house in two minutes. What I will say, though, is we are building a football club and the youngsters we have brought in will get better every year. You couldn't say that about the players last season because of their age.'

Hotte, at twenty-six, was the team's eldest player during the opening game of the season – a 0-0 home draw with Crawley, in which 'keeper Porter was not called on to make a single save. In the next match at Southport, O'Neill became the first player since the legendary Arthur Bottom to hit a hat-trick on his City debut. Bottom had managed the feat fifty-one years earlier and O'Neill's treble was also the first by a City player for more than nine years since Gary Bull went home with the match ball. McEwan's exciting side then moved up to second in the table following a 5-0 home win over Altrincham – their biggest margin of victory at Bootham Crescent since 1993. Prolific centre-back Dudgeon scored his third goal in three outings for the club and was joined on the sheet by O'Neill, Donaldson, Bishop and Stewart.

But the Minstermen missed out on a chance to go joint-top after nine matches when Scott Griffiths' ninety-fourth-minute equaliser cancelled out Donaldson's opening goal in a 1-1 draw. McEwan even revealed that prior to the match Sir Alex Ferguson, who the City boss worked for briefly at Manchester United, had called him to wish the team well. McEwan said, 'He rang to say he was pleased with what was happening and that he'd heard good things about us … He also gave me a rollicking because I had not told him before the start of the season how well the team were going to do and said that he would have backed us at 44-1. But you never know how well a team is going to gel and, as I keep saying, there's a very long way to go yet.'

After the team's attractive start to the season, though, McEwan cheekily suggested that, like Sir Alex, he was sent south of the border to educate the English about football. 'Billy Bremner, Kenny Dalglish and Bobby Collins were all brought down here to teach you lot how to play football and the master – Sir Alex Ferguson – is still in charge of Manchester United after eighteen years,' he smiled. 'There's a philosophy that, if you are winning, it doesn't matter how you play but I prefer a short, passing game. In every match, we want to treat our fans to a good game and reward them for spending their hard-earned cash. I'm a fan of football and I don't want to be bored to tears.'

Subsequently, the exciting Donaldson narrowly failed in a bid to equal a club record shared by Paul Aimson, Billy Fenton, Bottom and James Cowie when, having netted in six consecutive games, he was kept off the scoresheet in a 2-1 home victory over Canvey Island. But the squad's strength in depth suddenly came under scrutiny when centre-back Hotte, midfielder Panther and full-backs Peat and Price were all sidelined for long spells. City went on to concede a goal after eighty-seven minutes for the fifth time in their first thirteen games during a 2-2 draw against Gravesend and Northfleet, with future Minsterman Onome Sodje being responsible for the latest late equaliser. Those goals cost the team a total of seven points: without them, the club would have been five points clear at the top at that stage.

Following the eye-catching start to the campaign, McEwan also turned down overtures from a Football League club, believed to be Mansfield Town. Explaining the decision, he said, 'A League club wanted to chat with me about the possibility of being their manager, which is a compliment to the team, myself and York City Football Club. In the end, after a lot of thought, I decided it wouldn't be right.

'I have brought a lot of players to the football club and I owe it to the fans and players to stick with the team and help the club to be as successful as we can be. I've always said that the job here is a three-year one and I still believe that.'

As the injury problems intensified, Carlisle defender Lee Andrews, Grimsby midfielder Terry Barwick and Sheffield United left-back Evan Horwood were all drafted in on loan, while the search for new permanent employers for Brass continued with a loan switch from Harrogate to Southport. A bleak November, however, ended with the club failing to score for a full calendar month for only the second time in its history. Three defeats and a draw saw the Minstermen slip behind the play-off pace, and exit the FA Cup at home to high-flying Conference rivals Grays. An FA Trophy exit to Northwich followed in which Stockdale was replaced at half-time, with McEwan unhappy after the fledgling 'keeper conceded a penalty. The defeat took the Minstermen's winless run to eight matches.

McEwan also decided that the players would be training on 25 December, reasoning, 'You should wake up as a footballer thinking every day is Christmas Day because you are getting paid to do something you love doing. Our job is to entertain the people who are on holiday and there's plenty of time for the players to have holidays when they have sixteen weeks without a game in the summer.'

The decision seemed to pay off, as the team gained revenge for last season's 5-1 Boxing Day drubbing at local rivals Scarborough by beating the Seadogs 3-1 at KitKat Crescent – a result that underlined the progress made with McEwan at the helm. Midfielder Panther, who had been sidelined since the club's last league win over Canvey Island back in mid-October, inspired the team to victory after entering the action as a thirty-ninth-minute substitute. He immediately set up Bishop for an equaliser, following Brian Wake's opening goal, before Donaldson and McGurk added further goals after the break. City were denied a first-ever double over their North Yorkshire rivals, however, in the return match, when Chris Hughes grabbed a ninety-fifth-minute equaliser. Bishop scored both the visitors' goals in a 2-2 draw.

In mid-January, Brass finally departed the club for League Two Bury after reaching a settlement over the remaining eighteen months of his KitKat Crescent contract. Right-back Darren Craddock and striker Tcham N'Toya, meanwhile, were brought in on loan from Hartlepool and Chesterfield respectively to strengthen City during the transfer window, while Andrews, Pounder, Mallon and Horwood followed Brass out of the exit door. The first signs of a strained relationship between McEwan and star striker Bishop though, became evident following a dismal 2-0 defeat at Woking, where an over-hit Porter goal kick proved the visitors' only shot on target. Woking's goals were their first in a League game for three months. Singling out England C international Bishop, who he had fined earlier in the month for picking up a suspension for five bookings, McEwan said, 'We need more from our so-called international players because that's not good enough for York City. He got it with both barrels at half-time and full-time because I thought his performance was abysmal.'

On the back of a disappointing 0-0 home draw to Southport, Scarborough captain Neal Bishop was then signed in a good bit of deadline day business. The former double glazing fitter arrived for a 'small fee', as he became the club's first cash signing since Peter Duffield's £10,000 capture in June 2000. The club's 'Push for Promotion' appeal, set up after a £5,000 donation from supporter Michael Oglesby, had helped secure Bishop's services. It also emerged that Andy Bishop, out of contract at the end of that season, turned down a £20,000 deadline-day move to Bury after failing to agree personal terms. Both Bishops were, however, at the forefront of a fine February for the club, with a 3-1 victory at play-off contenders Exeter that saw the namesakes on the scoresheet alongside prolific centre-back Dudgeon, leading tough taskmaster McEwan to purr, 'I was really proud of the team and it was one of the best performances I have ever been associated with, and that's some statement because I have been involved with players at higher levels.'

A switch to 4-4-2 seemed to reap strong rewards for McEwan as Neal Bishop and Panther forged a strong central-midfield axis, while Donaldson and Bishop were looking potent as orthodox striking partners. McEwan won the February Manager of the Month award after four consecutive wins and Andy Bishop was named the Conference's Player of the Month. Bishop also became the first City player to score twenty goals in a season since Paul Barnes – a tally that included his first senior hat-trick in a 5-1 victory over Forest Green. He scored all three goals before the break, on his way to becoming the first man to claim a first-half treble for City since Paul Aimson thirty-four years earlier. Furthermore, there seemed to be a thawing in his frosty relationship with the manager, as McEwan said, 'His finishing was quality and I was pleased with him because he's working hard. He's got his fitness levels high and he's reaping the benefit.'

Having waited twenty-five months to complete a league double, the Minstermen then celebrated three within a week, following second wins of the campaign against Exeter, Tamworth and Forest Green. McEwan's men went on to become the first City side since Denis Smith's record-breaking 1983/84 team to enjoy six consecutive wins, a run that propelled them back into the play-off positions by mid-March. Another Dudgeon goal clinched the sixth victory in a 1-0 victory over Gravesend. The former Worksop defender's six goals over the course of the season were worth eight points to the team.

The players failed, however, in their attempt to equal the club record of seven successive wins, set in 1964/65, when a Porter mistake allowed Canvey Island to snatch a 1-1 home draw with their first on-target goal attempt seventy-six minutes into a windswept encounter in Essex. A controversial performance by referee Shaun Procter-Green in a 4-2 home defeat to champions-elect Accrington Stanley then saw McEwan attract an unlikely ally in former referee instructor Eddie Benson. The Gainsborough official incurred the wrath of home supporters when he awarded a penalty against Price for supposed deliberate handball, and then waved away spot-kick protests at the other end after Andy Bishop was shoved over in the box. Benson said afterwards, 'I've always defended the decisions of referees in the local or professional game and have consistently adopted this view much to the annoyance of my fellow York City supporters. Unfortunately, I witnessed the worst two referee decisions I can remember on Saturday. It was the worst referee's display I have seen and I am quite sure the assessor would have taken a similar view.'

McEwan was even more scathing in his assessment of Proctor-Green's performance when he blasted, 'We got done by an official who nearly caused me to walk out of the ground in disgust because of his decisions. It was an absolutely disgraceful and abysmal performance and I told him after the game that he would be getting no marks from me at all. It's a waste of time when idiots like him spoil the game.'

City climbed back into the play-off positions, though, with a 3-0 win at Altrincham in early April, during which Donaldson (2) and Andy Bishop shared the goals.

But the Minstermen's promotion hopes were eventually extinguished after two defeats over the Easter holiday. A Hotte own goal, described by McEwan as 'Mickey Mouse', and a red card for Nathan Peat, who was labelled 'stupid' by the livid Minstermen chief, contributed to a 2-0 defeat at Cambridge on Good Friday. On Easter Monday, the team were then defeated 2-0 at home to Halifax. Porter made a mistake for the visitors' first goal and O'Neill went on to miss two good chances, before ex-City midfielder Steve Bushell secured victory for the Shaymen late on. A drained McEwan kicked every ball during an amazingly demonstrative display on the touchline. He performed an amusing – if ill-advised – role reversal by shoving the fourth official back towards the players' tunnel, offered the referee his spectacles, and got embroiled in an angry argument with an abusive home supporter towards the end of the game, which led to the perpetrator of the altercation leaving the ground. Afterwards, the passionate City boss ranted:

> It's early days in the rebuilding of this football club. Three years ago, we were in administration and at this stage last season we were fighting relegation. This season, with three games left to go, we were on the verge of a play-off position. We have taken the club to dizzy heights in a short period of time and I think our real fans understand that but one doesn't and I had him thrown out of the ground.
>
> He said the team was crap. He's entitled to his opinion, but do I have to deal with idiots like that? We have got turned over by a good team and had indifferent results in the last six games but it upset me when that guy came to the dugout and gave me a mouthful. I couldn't believe it. I thought what's the use if I have fans like that? But I know he's only one guy. He needs to think how disappointed I feel, the rest of the team feel and the real York City faithful feel.
>
> What this club has achieved in a short space of time is miraculous. It's taken Accrington Stanley about forty-four years to get back into the League, it took Doncaster five years and Halifax, Hereford and Exeter still haven't managed it.
>
> Last season we were a laughing stock, and easy fodder for teams like Canvey Island. Now, we are a tough outfit, but our little team was never going to be an overnight success.

McEwan also pointed to the club's poor financial condition as part of his call for greater understanding of his task at KitKat Crescent. 'We are trying to get in the League but you need money to improve the squad and, let's face facts, there's not a penny in the club,' he reasoned. 'Accrington have got money, we've got KitKats. I'd love to spend money and have a list in my drawer of players I would like to bring to York City next week, but it's not possible on our wage budget.'

City's inability to compete with the division's leading lights in 2005/06 was ultimately illustrated by a failure to beat any of the top six teams during the season, as league runners-up Hereford clinched a 3-1 win at KitKat Crescent on the final day. In total, McEwan's team managed just three points from a possible thirty-six against those sides and finished the campaign eighth. The manager was still pleased with his players' efforts, saying, 'I have nothing but praise for the boys and I think they have been fantastic. They have surpassed my expectations as twelve months ago we were celebrating staying up.'

McEwan was left reeling, though, by the Football League's rejection of the club's appeal against the complete withdrawal of funding for York's Centre of Excellence programme after two years as a Conference outfit. It served as another financial blow for the Minstermen and McEwan even enlisted the help of Sir Alex Ferguson, who benefited from City's youth policy when he bought Bootham Crescent graduate Jonathan Greening for a seven-figure sum for Manchester United. McEwan said, 'Alex Ferguson understands this club has a reputation for development and a proud tradition of producing young players but, now the club has fallen on hard times, there does not seem to be any sympathy from certain areas towards our football club. There's an attitude of those are the rules and that's it.'

In spite of the club's financial battles, however, McEwan had restored pride in York's football team. Following two dreadful seasons in front of goal, the team scored more goals in 2005/06 than any City side since 1995, when Paul Barnes was still leading the line and Richard Cresswell was waiting in the wings to fill his boots. Andy Bishop (twenty-five) and Clayton Donaldson (eighteen) had plundered the lion's share of the goals and the prospects for the prolific pair during the next season were mouth-watering.

Sadly, though, they had played their last game together.

Left: Centre of Excellence graduate David Stockdale, who was released by Billy McEwan before becoming a future Premier League goalkeeper and England squad member. (*The Press* staff photographer)

Below: Clayton Donaldson claims the second goal against Scarborough. (Garry Atkinson)

Andy Bishop opens the scoring against Scarborough during the 3-1 Boxing Day win in 2005. (Garry Atkinson)

3

'BOB SHANKLY WOULD BE TURNING IN HIS GRAVE'

Ever wondered about the best way to end a fractious relationship?

Well, in the summer of 2006, Andy Bishop decided walking away was the best option.

Despite their dual presence at Bootham Crescent having been of mutual benefit to both manager and top scorer, Billy McEwan and Bishop never seemed far away from their next fall-out. Perhaps then, Bishop signing for Bury without consulting McEwan, after turning down a new deal with the Minstermen, should have come as no surprise. There was also even more galling news, though, when it emerged that, despite him being twenty-three, the club would not be entitled to a transfer fee for Bishop, as would normally be expected under the Bosman ruling. A clause had been inserted in Bishop's contract when he signed for the Minstermen, effectively allowed him to leave for free at the end of his two-year deal. In the aftermath, McEwan questioned Bishop's ambition, saying, 'I can't believe he's signed for Bury. No disrespect, but I don't see that as a career-enhancing move. If he had stayed with me another year, I could have made him a better player and got him a bigger club. We've worked hard on him and he's doubled his goal tally this season. I'm proud of that, because he's not the easiest to work with. I understand he wants to be a Football League player but, if he's ambitious, then why sign for a club struggling to stay in it?

'We understand, however, that he's had a super offer and there's no way we would have matched it. We would have needed to sell a stand to keep him.'

One of the most emotive issues in the club's history, meanwhile, dominated the rest of the summer. The club's fans were asked to vote on whether they should relinquish ownership of their club to managing director Jason McGill's Malton-based company JM Packaging, who already owned a 15 per cent interest in the Minstermen. A special general meeting was held at the Barbican by the Supporters' Trust, the club's 85 per cent majority shareholders. It was reported that the club had failed to meet the first £100,000 loan repayment to the Football Stadia Improvement Fund. Furthermore, City finance director Terry Doyle had also told JM Packaging that their £300,000 loan to the club was unlikely to be paid back by the January 2007 deadline.

A proposal was put forward by JM Packaging to invest a further £650,000 into the club after exchanging the £300,000 loan for a 75 per cent – plus one share – majority shareholding in the club. The £650,000 was intended to cover £150,000 in losses initially, with the remainder used to provide annual £100,000 injections for the next five years. It was also proposed that the loan would be provided at a rate of 11 per cent interest but only the interest would be repayable – and not the loaned money – on an assumed future sale of Bootham Crescent. McGill would later waive the interest payments and only ask back what he had put into the club on a pound-for-pound basis.

A spate of Supporters' Trust board members resigned from their positions in the build-up to the meeting, with many against the transferral of shares amid accusations of being misled. In opposition, The Friends of Bootham Crescent, a supporters' body formed when former chairman Douglas Craig threatened to evict the club, were against any dilution of the Trust's ownership, with spokesman David Allison saying, 'Given the tortuous recent history of the club, it is vital that we remain in collective ownership. There is a moral issue here. We are a Trust-run club and that means the ownership of the club cannot and should not ever fall into one person's hands.' Crucially, protections were put in place to prevent the ground being switched away from club ownership again. A £200,000 loan, meanwhile, from a group headed by former Trust board member Mike Grant, which would enable the Trust to maintain their 85 per cent shareholding, was considered unworkable and an insufficient investment to keep the club going by the Trust. Manager Billy McEwan added his weight to the takeover, saying:

> I understand fans not wanting to give up ownership of the club but he [McGill] has financial clout and, importantly, York City at heart. Our fans are fantastic and the Trust have done a great job saving the club but it's not easy to keep running it on a shoestring. No big companies have come forward to offer the kind of money Jason has done, and where is it going to come from otherwise? Bills are still coming in and need paying.
>
> He's prepared to put his money in to help the club. He doesn't have to do that and, if he doesn't, where's York City going to go and where's Billy McEwan going to go because I won't hang around if I haven't got a penny to spend on players.
>
> I would have to consider my future if the vote went the other way. His involvement in the club was a reason why I came to York City. I have been impressed with his work for the club, as I have been by the rest of the board. His support for the club has been fantastic since I have been here and he's even helped entice players.
>
> He's a young, forward-thinking managing director who has plans for the future that he wants to implement. Jason and his family are York fans through and through, he is prepared to back the club and we need his money behind us.

The motion was eventually passed by a 78 per cent majority, ushering in a new era at Bootham Crescent.

Darren Craddock, meanwhile, arrived on a permanent deal after a successful loan spell from Hartlepool earlier in the year. Darlington went on to announce that they wanted to keep last season's City loan star David McGurk, and Bury and Bristol Rovers also declared an interest in his services, but he made a permanent move to York on the same day his old Middlesbrough school pal Craig Farrell also put pen to paper. Having played the whole of the 2005/06 season without anybody over the age of thirty, McEwan also signed his first-ever thirty-something when super-fit floor-fitter Steve Bowey – a veteran of thirty-one years – agreed terms. McEwan also recruited experienced goalkeeper Tom Evans from Scunthorpe after releasing both David Stockdale and Chris Porter. Stockdale was saved from the soccer scrapheap when a successful trial saw him taken on as a No. 2 at then Football League outfit Darlington. After incurring the wrath of McEwan, who criticised him for gaining weight during his final season at Bootham Crescent, Stockdale was determined to make a go of his second chance, saying, 'I have got back into shape after letting myself go at York. I accept now that was the case and agree with the manager, but I would have preferred not to have been criticised in public. It has probably given me a kick up the backside though to get me going again and I feel a better person now. I would have loved to have stayed at York because I was there for a long time and have a great affection for the club.'

Former Manchester United trainee Ross Greenwood and full-back Anthony Lloyd were other additions before the start of the season.

Having been in play-off contention until the penultimate game of the 2005/06 campaign, McEwan's target for the new season was simply to improve on that effort. Following an opening day 0-0 home draw with Exeter, the Minstermen racked up four successive wins against Stevenage, Gravesend, Burton and Rushden, briefly going top of the table at one stage. It proved the only time the Bootham Crescent club would occupy such a lofty perch during the Conference era. Billy McEwan went on to win the August Manager of the Month award, jointly awarded to him with Frank Gray and Jim Smith at Grays and Oxford respectively.

A 0-0 home draw with Stafford followed, which was notable for the debut of Martyn Woolford, plucked by McEwan from Frickley Athletic. The team's six-game undefeated start to the campaign – the longest in twenty-two years – then ended when Evans was sent off after sixteen minutes at Crawley and the Minstermen went down 3-0. In the FA Cup, City squeezed past Newcastle Benfield Bay Plastics 1-0 – a game that brought raw centre-forward Richard Brodie to McEwan's attention. Benfield's Brodie – a trainee joiner – gave City centre-backs Jason Goodliffe and Luke Foster, who were no shrinking violets themselves, a bruising time.

McEwan's players later gave a good account of themselves in a 1-0 home defeat to League One high-fliers Bristol City, who snatched a first-round proper win through Jamie McCombe's header – one of the visitors' two on-target goal attempts. A test of the team's title credentials was also provided by the visit to Bootham Crescent of league leaders Dagenham. McEwan, though, was left seething when the Essex visitors arrived late after their 10 a.m. train from London was delayed. The game kicked off an hour late, by which time some City fans had gone home, and McEwan also claimed that Craddock's pre-match hamstring injury could have been caused by the constant warming up and down. 'For them to turn up at that time is disgraceful,' he blasted after watching his team lose 3-2. 'You can't leave yourself wide open to the risk of a train arriving on time … They should have been sent back on the train and that would have been their punishment – coming back to play the game in midweek.'

Speculation, meanwhile, began to grow about the future of Clayton Donaldson, who had taken over the star striker mantle from Bishop. Having quickly acquired the nickname Donaldinho, especially for his exploits in the team's yellow-and-blue away strip, the player insisted his head would not be turned by transfer talk. 'I don't read too much into the speculation,' he claimed in December. 'I've heard it before and nothing has happened so I will just keep my head down and enjoy my football until a point comes when the manager or board come and tell me they have had an offer they want to consider. Obviously, if a big club came in for me, and it was the right move for me and the club, I would have to consider it because I want to further my career and play at a decent level, but I'm happy at York.'

To avoid extra policing costs, the club decided not to play at Bootham Crescent on Boxing Day, but then staged Fight Night three days later in an extraordinary contest against Woking. The game's flashpoint came when James Dudgeon, warming up as a substitute, attempted to step in as a peacemaker when Neal Bishop got in a tangle with visiting left-back Danny Bunce. Woking coach Matt Crossley then dashed 20 yards from the visitors' dugout to perform his interpretation of an old festive favourite – *The Nutcracker* – on Dudgeon, headbutting the York defender.

A massive melee followed, with players and officials from both benches involved, and Nathan Peat, who had been substituted earlier, threw a flurry of punches. All three were shown red cards, despite not being actively involved in the game at the time, and Woking, almost incidentally, won with their only on-target shot of the night from Jamie Taylor on eighty-one minutes. 'In all my forty years in the game I have never been associated with anything like that,' said a shell-shocked McEwan afterwards. The incident later led to a fine of £2,000 for the club following an FA conduct charge of failing to control their players. Peat was found guilty of violent conduct, as was Crossley, while Dudgeon was found guilty of improper conduct.

There was a happier start to the New Year when the Minstermen won 3-1 at Morecambe, courtesy of Donaldson, Farrell and Bowey goals, having lost on each of their previous three trips to Christie Park. Donaldon bagged a brace in the next match during a 5-0 win against Crawley to reach twenty goals for the season by 6 January. In the following game, however, he received the first red card of his career for leading with his elbow in a 2-1 defeat at Kidderminster, earning him a three-match ban. During his enforced lay-off, news then broke that Donaldson had signed a pre-contract agreement to move to Hibernian at the end of the season.

Equally as big a blow was the revelation that, as with Andy Bishop in the summer, the club would not receive a penny for his transfer, as the age a player was entitled to a Bosman ruling free transfer in Scotland was a year younger than in England at the time. City had earlier turned down a six-figure sum from Scunthorpe, a £100,000 bid from Peterborough and a £25,000 derisory offer from Accrington Stanley for his services, having placed a £500,000 price on his head. Hibs subsequently offered £50,000 to take him straight away, with twenty-one-year-old striker Sam Morrow also put forward in a loan swap deal until the end of the season. However, the Minstermen decided to keep Donaldson until the end of the season.

Jason McGill described the news as 'absolutely devastating' and it also left McEwan 'totally disillusioned with football'. McEwan went on to throw a Scottish newspaper photographer out of the ground after he had arrived to picture Donaldson. The York manager was also further incensed by the fact that Donaldson's agent, Andy Sprott, was the same man who represented Bishop during his move to Bury.

York did not win any of their fixtures during Donaldson's suspension, which ended following a 2-0 home defeat to Tamworth, whose captain Adie Smith lit up a celebratory cigarette as he left Bootham Crescent. It might as well have been a cigar, such was the ease with which the visitors secured maximum points, as Tamworth manager Gary Mills enjoyed the first win of his second spell in charge of the Lambs.

On Donaldson's return, however, the Minstermen registered their biggest away win in twelve years when they hammered hosts Altrincham 4-0. Donaldson did not net, but nineteen-year-old substitute Brodie, recruited in the wake of the Hibernian bombshell, marked his debut with a goal, and also set one up for Woolford. Bishop and Bowey had scored earlier in the first half. Prior to a 1-0 home win over Weymouth, McEwan was left reeling again, though, after an audacious request from Hibs further soured the livid manager's love for a club he once played for. 'I can't believe they had the cheek to send us an email asking for two free tickets and a car park pass,' McEwan blasted. 'They wanted to see Clayton Donaldson play but they can pay our little club after taking him for nothing. Hibs were my No. 1 club and I am sure their old manager Bob Shankly [the brother of legendary former Liverpool manager Bill] would be turning in his grave if he knew what was happening at the club.'

At the end of February, City went down 2-1 at Dagenham, which all but ended the visitors' hopes of automatic promotion as they slipped fifteen points behind the champions-elect.

The team were generally stronger on their travels, with drainage problems at Bootham Crescent not always creating a playing surface conducive to McEwan's favoured passing game. Following a 2-1 home win over Northwich, though, McEwan was left incandescent after some supporters booed off his trailing team at half-time. He reasoned, 'If we were where Halifax are now then I might understand but that worries me as well because, you never know, we might be there next year or the year after and what happens then? Does that make me a bad manager?' His words would prove prophetic in a matter of months, however unlikely they sounded at the time.

Donaldson then ended seven matches without a goal by hitting a hat-trick in a 5-0 victory at Cambridge, equalling the biggest away league win in the club's history. Farrell and on-loan defender Janos Kovacs also netted. Back-to-back home defeats and a run of two points from twelve, though, threatened to derail the team's play-off push before an Easter weekend 2-1 win at fellow top-five contenders Burton. Woolford and Farrell were the marksmen. A subsequent 1-0 triumph at Southport, courtesy of Donaldson's penalty, saw the side equal a club record of thirteen away wins in a league season, emulating Denis Smith's all-conquering 1983/84 team. Bishop's goal against Oxford in the final game of the regular season went on to secure a play-off place. Needing a point to be sure, McEwan's men won 1-0. City went into the play-offs as the form team with McEwan having carried off another Manager of the Month award for an April in which his players claimed four wins and a draw.

But bookmakers could not split City, and their semi-final opponents Morecambe and the first leg at Bootham Crescent ended goalless. The hosts dominated, with Craig James seeing a free-kick saved, Bowey missing the target twice and Shrimps 'keeper Steven Drench saving from Woolford and Manny Panther. Morecambe winger Wayne Curtis arguably missed the best chance of the game, though, when he fired over the bar from 2 yards on seventy-three minutes. Curtis was not as profligate in the second leg as Morecambe went on to become one of the first two club teams to play at the newly developed Wembley stadium, following a 2-1 win on the coast. The visitors, who had not conceded a goal in more than seven hours of football, shipped two in seven minutes – both scored by the bustling Curtis. York had earlier drawn first blood when Bowey converted a twentieth-minute penalty after Drench had clattered into Donaldson. Both players were injured following the clash, with Drench stretchered off, to be replaced by substitute shot-stopper Scott Davies. Donaldson, meanwhile, laboured on before making way for Brodie on seventy-seven minutes.

The tie's turning point came on the stroke of half-time when left-back James was penalised for climbing on Morecambe winger Paul Lloyd. Adam Yates then swung in a free-kick that tempted Evans off his line, only for the City 'keeper to quickly realise that he was not going to reach the cross. With Evans left stranded, Curtis headed into the unguarded goal and, two minutes into the second period, the hosts forged in front. Evans saved two shots from Curtis but, with the third, the Shrimps winger lifted the ball over the City 'keeper, as well as the covering defenders who had retreated towards the goal line. City tried to get back into the match, but a tame 20-yard Bishop effort was the only shot on target the visitors could muster other than Bowey's penalty. At the final whistle, though, McEwan had nothing but praise for his side's efforts and also paid tribute to Donaldson following his farewell appearance, saying, 'He will be a big loss but we wish him well because he's been a great kid to work with. He's stuck more than forty goals in during two years and has given our fans a lot of pleasure and entertainment. If we had not had him, we would not have got as far as we have done and he will be a very hard act to follow.'

The Minstermen chief again referenced Yorkshire rivals Halifax, though, when he turned his attention to the following season. 'We are hurting at the moment but we will come back in the summer and try to improve on this season,' he promised. 'It's a big ask but we will be trying. We don't want to do what Halifax did. They have had a poor season after getting to the play-off final.'

Clayton Donaldson challenges Morecambe defender Chris Blackburn for possession during the 2007 play-off semi-final first leg. (David Harrison)

A confident Neal Bishop gives fans the thumbs up after honours end even following the 2007 play-off semi-final first leg. (David Harrison)

Martyn Woolford and Morecambe's Jim Bentley contest the ball during the play-off semi-final clash at Bootham Crescent. (David Harrison)

McEwan consoles defender Daniel Parslow at Morecambe after the Minstermen's 2007 play-off quest ends following a 2-1 aggregate defeat. (Frank Dwyer)

An injured Donaldson bids farewell to York supporters after the Morecambe match, having agreed pre-contract terms with Hibernian. (Frank Dwyer)

4

'THE PINNACLE OF MY COACHING CAREER'

Teetotal Billy McEwan never had a problem with hangovers until the start of the 2007/08 season, but providing a remedy for the club's Morecambe disappointment would prove more troublesome that he could have feared.

The manager initially raised a few eyebrows when he released eight players after the play-off defeat with Steve Bowey, Mark Convery, Nathan Peat, Anthony Lloyd and James Dudgeon among the surprise departures. Lloyd was later brought back to the club at the end of September after working in a warehouse during the intervening period. Midfielder Convery questioned the manager's shake-up at the time, saying, 'If the same team had been kept I think we would have a better chance of winning the League next season but he must have made his mind up that if you don't finish champions a lot of changes must be made. Time will tell whether that's the right thing to do.'

Having lost Donaldson a year after Andy Bishop decided to seek pastures new, McEwan then suffered another blow when the previous season's Supporters' and Players' Player of the Year Neal Bishop moved to League Two Barnet after rejecting new terms at Bootham Crescent. The move infuriated McEwan, who reasoned that then Barnet boss Paul Fairclough should have relinquished his role as manager of the England C team that Bishop was capped by. 'I don't think it's right,' McEwan argued. 'He's a club manager and he's getting to work with these players at close quarters. He can get a good look at them and get to know them.'

McEwan's rebuilding programme saw him recruit left-back Mark Robinson from Torquay, Ebbsfleet striker Onome Sodje, Northwich pair Stuart Elliott and Paul Brayson, Rushden & Diamonds striker Chris Beardsley, Hartlepool midfielder Phil Turnbull, Chester midfielder Alex Meechan and Hartlepool defender Carl Jones. Elliott, aged twenty-nine, incredibly made City the twenty-sixth club of his nomadic career, which had included spells on the books of Arsenal and Newcastle, as well as the likes of Harrow Borough, Durham City and Waltham Forest. McEwan missed out on Leicester City teenager Andy King, though, after he played as a trialist for the Minstermen during a 5-0 victory over Sheffield FC. King's agent advised the future Wales international and Championship regular against a loan move to Bootham Crescent. Optimism was still high on the eve of the new campaign, however, with skipper Manny Panther declaring, 'We've got the best team spirit in the dressing room since I've been here.'

But the opening-day home match with Cambridge did not go as planned. A disappointing afternoon saw debutant Elliott sent off during a 2-1 defeat. Elliott struck out at Leo Fortune-West in the penalty box to receive his marching orders, giving Lee Boylan the opportunity to win the match from the spot. McEwan fined his new midfielder and ordered him to train with the youth team, while the rest of the side travelled to Burton for their next match. Ten-man Burton delivered another blow when they fought back from 3-1 down with eighty-two minutes on the clock to clinch a highly unlikely victory on a terrible night for City's defence and struggling 'keeper Evans.

Following a 1-1 draw at Exeter, a 2-0 home defeat to Forest Green Rovers left the team with just one point from twelve. But Brayson then secured the team's first win of the season with a stoppage-time volley at his old club Northwich.

Before the transfer window closed, Derry City defender Darren Kelly and Barnsley midfielder Nicky Wroe were then brought in to bolster the ranks.

But the Minstermen marked their seventy-fifth anniversary at Bootham Crescent with a 3-2 home defeat to Rushden & Diamonds, losing in front of their own fans for a third consecutive game for the first time in the Conference era. An irritable McEwan refused to let the Setanta Sports television cameras in the home dressing rooms during the half-time interval. Afterwards, teenager Stephen Henderson was brought in on loan from Bristol City to replace Evans, but City continued to ship goals, with their one-time misfiring striker Joe O'Neill earning new club Altrincham a 2-2 draw with an injury-time header.

Chants of 'What A Load Of Rubbish' and 'You Don't Know What You're Doing' from the away end then followed during a 3-0 defeat at Kidderminster to illustrate how quickly McEwan's stock had plummeted at the club. Afterwards, the dejected manager said, 'The supporters are unhappy, but nobody is as frustrated and disappointed as I am. I hate it, but that's my job.'

> We've had a couple of decent seasons, particularly the last one, and at the moment we're having a difficult one, but you don't become a bad manager because the team's not winning. We've not done too badly in the previous hundred games. We can't keep harking back though. It's what's happening now that's the most concerning thing and this team is not playing as well as I expect it to play.

Another former City striker Rob Elvins, who failed to net in nine matches while at Bootham Crescent, rubbed more salt into the wounds when the league's pacesetters Aldershot secured a flattering 2-0 home win over McEwan's side. It left the team with just the one win against Northwich from their opening ten games but McEwan remained defiant, saying, 'I've given my life to York City for the last two-and-a-half years and given total commitment.'

> It would be the easy option to walk away, but why would I want someone else to come in and take the credit for this team? The club has been transformed over the last two years. We are struggling now, but I will never hang up my coat and walk out. We're like a boxer on the ropes at the moment, but we have got to keep getting back up because the guy that falls to the floor is a loser.

A tempestuous clash at Grays saw City eventually get their second triumph of the season. Victory came at a cost, though, with striker Beardsley suffering a broken jaw in two places after a clash with home defender Jamie Stuart. The incident saw Stuart sent off with a penalty also awarded to the visitors. Robinson and Richard Brodie later received their marching orders too. Robinson's afternoon proved only slightly less agonising than Bearsdley's, after he had a penalty saved prior to the professional foul that saw him red carded. Sodje netted after Stuart's dismissal, while Elliott doubled the lead while it was ten *v.* ten. City then saw the game out with nine men after Brodie was ordered off on seventy-four minutes following a tussle with Stuart Thurgood.

Beardsley ended up with three plates inserted into his jaw, leading Essex Police to launch an investigation. But the flashpoint was not caught on camera and, although Stuart was later arrested and charged with grievous bodily harm, he was acquitted a year later.

Fortunes appeared to be turning temporarily as the Minstermen ended a sixteen-year wait to record a win in front of live television cameras. Alex Meechan scored the winning goal in a 3-2 home victory over Halifax with the club having lost six and drawn three of their previous encounters on the square screen. It was the second of four wins in six matches but that run had a big blemish with part-timers Histon enjoying a 4-1 victory at Bootham Crescent – City's fifth defeat in seven home matches. The last two victories of that six-game sequence, however, saw City keep back-to-back clean sheets against Stafford (2-0) and Woking (3-0).

The hope was that lessons were being learned following a record of seventeen goals conceded during the team's first seven fixtures, when defending set pieces proved particularly problematic. A return of ten York goals in two matches then came just a fortnight before McEwan was sacked. First, FA Cup fourth qualifying round visitors Rushall Olympic were seen off 6-0 as the club enjoyed their biggest win since 1985. Looking at the condition of certain Rushall players, however, it would have come as no surprise if a fight had broken out in the visitors' dressing room over who claimed the size 38-inch shorts prior to kick off.

The result against such poor opposition flattered the home side, with only a Sodje goal separating the teams after seventy minutes. Sodje then doubled the Minstermen's lead before substitute Craig Farrell grabbed a tenth-minute hat-trick on his return after a seven-week injury lay-off. Farrell then went on to set up the final goal for Wroe.

City next racked up a sixth victory in nine matches by winning 4-1 at Farsley Celtic. Farrell came off the bench again to blast in two more late goals after earlier efforts from Brayson and loan signing Daniel McBreen. Back-to-back home defeats against FA Cup opponents Havant & Waterlooville (1-0) and Salisbury (3-1) would spell the end for McEwan, however.

After the Havant defeat, McEwan lambasted his players, saying, 'The whole team should look at themselves in the mirror and say "hang on a minute, why have we been beaten by an amateur team?" We've been beaten by an amateur team because we've probably underestimated them. Not me, them in the dressing room. Only they can answer.' McEwan then labelled Craddock 'brainless', after the Salisbury defeat, substituting the right-back seven minutes into the second half after a reckless challenge while he was on a yellow card. 'Keeper Evans was also culpable for all three of the visitors' goals.

A resigned McEwan put his fate in the board's hands afterwards, saying, 'It's a very frustrating job at the moment. I feel for the fans coming and paying their hard-earned cash to see the team get beaten and, aside from one or two moans, I thought they were great in general. There's not much else I can do. I'm trying my best and the players are trying their best. If I'm not good enough, then they will have to get somebody else in if they can do a better job. It's up to them, but sixteen points from eight games was a great haul going into this game.'

In a board statement two days later, the board announced that McEwan had been relieved of his duties 'with regret' before adding to 'allow the present circumstances to continue would be a disservice to the club and our supporters'. The team were nineteenth in the table after nineteen games and communications director Sophie McGill later added, 'It was clear that something was inherently wrong when you see the passionless performances there have been in the last two games at KitKat Crescent.'

Reflecting on his mentor's swift fall from grace, captain Panther admitted, 'It is a remarkable game sometimes. When we had 7,000 at KitKat Crescent for the play-offs, who would have thought things would go so bad?' But, having lost his air of invincibility, McEwan had also lost his job. Typically, he left with a parting shot, saying, 'I told the chairman two and a half years ago, I will do all the spadework and someone else will get the rewards. To a point, I have been a victim of my own success. But there can be no excuses. We gave bad goals away and Tom Evans was not a patch on the player he was last year. I'm still going to have a bet on the team getting into the top ten though.'

In the wake of McEwan's dismissal, Colin Walker became caretaker manager with the team having lost eight of their twelve matches at Bootham Crescent during 2007/08. The former New Zealand international immediately made it clear that he would be interested in the role on a permanent basis, saying, 'I've been under some good managers in the past and, when an opportunity presents itself, even unfortunately through circumstances that are sad, you may only get the one chance, so yes I want the job. For me, my managerial style is going to be about the two Fs – firm, but fair. The way I have taken the reserves is I have let the players express themselves a little more and hopefully that might just be the thing that gets them going. I have never been in this position before but I am really, really looking forward to it.'

Striker Farrell spoke of the players' respect for the new boss, saying, 'Colin and Billy are totally different people. They go about the job in a totally different way. I really like Colin, all the players do, and we are all behind him. I think Colin is more laid back than Billy. They both have good attributes. We are looking to express ourselves a bit more on the pitch. The way Billy wanted us to play, sometimes I think we took a bit too much notice and didn't express ourselves.'

Prior to taking charge of his first game at Weymouth, Walker admitted that 'it is going to be the pinnacle of my coaching career.'

Making personnel and tactical changes for the South Coast clash, Walker dropped senior professional Elliott and recalled Daniel Parslow as he switched to a 3-5-2 formation, in which Martyn Woolford was given a roaming central role, behind the front two. The under-fire Evans went on to save a penalty during a 2-1 win, secured by Kelly and Farrell goals. A celebratory huddle, including Walker, unused substitutes and other travelling members of the squad, took place at the final whistle, suggesting a harmony between players and management that had reportedly eroded under McEwan.

City went on to triumph 2-1 at Ebbsfleet, with Sodje enjoying a dream return to his former club, scoring an eleventh goal of the season before he hit the post with a second chance that Woolford followed up to net. A 3-1 FA Trophy win at Altrincham carried on the momentum as goals from Farrell, Lloyd and Wroe saw the team equal a club record of five consecutive away wins.

Seventy-two City fans then braved freezing conditions the Saturday before Christmas to watch a goalless ninety minutes at Stafford in the Setanta Shield – a competition about as fashionable as a Yuletide jumper your Gran might knit you. Conference general manager Dennis Strudwick did nothing to raise the competition's profile either, with the underwhelming announcement that the final would take place at 'a Blue Square Premier ground at the very least'. Extra-time goals from Brodie and Sodje, though, meant City managed a sixth straight away win to take their place outright in the history books. Walker went on to land the manager's job on a permanent basis following a 2-1 Boxing Day victory over Droylsden, courtesy of Farrell's penalty and a Kelly header.

It was the fifth win during his six-match undefeated spell as caretaker manager and a hastily-prepared club statement read, 'The board have been impressed with the attitude, aptitude and professionalism shown by Colin during recent weeks and the positive response to his approach shown by the players.' Sophie McGill added, 'When the players were told about Colin's appointment in the dressing room they were all delighted. Not only do we have a very professional person, but we also have a nice personality that the players, media and board of directors can work with. For the first time in a really long time, I feel the club is really united and everybody is pulling in the same direction. Colin's really helped to raise players' morale. They are playing for him and we believe that's important and that he's the right man to take York City forward.'

A 2-0 home win against Weymouth with goals from David McGurk and Woolford then saw Walker set another club record. He became the first City manager to end a calendar year with five straight wins and also picked up the Conference Manager of the Month award for December. As predicted by McEwan, the team had also climbed into the table's top ten positions. An incredible game at Droylsden on New Year's Day then ended 4-3 in the visitors' favour, despite the hosts going 3-2 in front in the eighty-ninth minute. Super-sub Brodie, who earlier had a hand in goals for Panther and Farrell on eighty-seven minutes, pounced twice in stoppage time to secure a sixth successive win and seventh consecutive away victory, sending a 531-strong travelling army of fans delirious. The visitors also hit the bar three times and had a hat-trick of penalty shouts rejected during a remarkable match.

The win meant Walker had made the most successful start to a managerial career at Bootham Crescent of any other man in the club's history. His eight-match undefeated beginning beat the previous record, held by 1960s chief Tom Lockie. A cautionary note to anybody getting overly excited, though, was provided by the fact that six of City's seven wins under Walker had come against bottom-six sides.

During the January transfer window, Northwich midfielder Simon Rusk became Walker's first signing, and former Scarborough defender Jimmy Beadle arrived soon afterwards. In the FA Trophy, the Minstermen progressed to the third round by winning 4-1 at a Grays team, boasting the Conference's second-best defensive record. Wroe (two), Woolford and Brodie scored the goals, with the latter pair forging a strong striking partnership after being thrown together by Walker. Both were on target again as City swept aside champions-in-waiting Aldershot 2-0 at Bootham Crescent, where the visitors managed just one shot on target all afternoon.

Walker then offloaded Beardsley and Brayson, while recruiting veteran targetman Fortune-West, who joined the Minstermen on loan from Cambridge before the transfer window closed. Walker's undefeated managerial reign eventually came to an end, though, following his fifteenth game at the helm – a penalty shoot-out defeat to Northwich in the Setanta Shield. But a 2-2 draw at Halifax saw City break yet another record, set by the 1955 FA Cup semi-final team, when they went a thirteenth away match without defeat. That run ended with a first league defeat under Walker, as his team went down 3-1 at Histon.

But an FA Trophy semi-final place was secured soon afterwards when Parslow celebrated the end of a week in which he captained Wales' semi-professional team against England by netting his first-ever senior goal for City to see off Rushden & Diamonds 1-0. With all focus now firmly switching to the Trophy, City suffered a blow when they lost their semi-final, first-leg tie at Torquay 2-0. Strikers Tim Sills and Lee Phillips were the hosts' marksmen, but the outcome could have been different with Elliott rattling the crossbar and Sodje missing a stoppage-time sitter. In the second leg, Chris Todd's own goal reduced the aggregate deficit, but City could not level the tie, with Sodje having an effort wrongly disallowed for offside and Robinson and Woolford seeing strong penalty appeals turned down.

Defeat meant missing out on an estimated £400,000 windfall, and more bad news followed when the club admitted defeat in its plans to relocate to land adjacent to Nestlé's Wigginton Road factory. Jason McGill, now club chairman, added that time and financial constraints also made the geographically-appealing York Central site an unviable option too, with land costing £2 million an acre and the development expected to take a further fifteen years to complete.

With only league respectability left to play for, City ended the season sloppily and the set-piece fallibility that dogged the side's start to the campaign returned with a vengeance. Having been undefeated in nine home matches, Walker's team lost to Ebbsfleet (1-0), Woking (3-2) and Oxford (1-0) at Bootham Crescent in quick succession. The Woking defeat saw rookie referee Ross Joyce send off three City players, with Craddock, Elliott and Evans all given their marching orders. The home side finished the game with eight men. A season's nadir was then reached when the team were thumped 6-1 at Crawley with young rookie Josh Mimms enduring a nightmare between the sticks after being preferred to Evans. The Minstermen signed off at home, though, with their biggest league win of the campaign at Bootham Crescent, defeating Farsley Celtic 4-1 to relegate the Leeds side.

Despite being told his services would not be needed the following season, along with others such as skipper Panther, Craddock and Elliott, Evans surprisingly started the last game of the season at Salisbury, who went on to score three unanswered goals from crosses into his 6-yard box. It meant York ended the season with just two wins from their last eleven games although a club record of five players – Woolford, Sodje, Brodie, Farrell and Wroe – finished the campaign on double figures for goals.

Panther, such a talismanic figure under McEwan, admitted the moment was right to move on, having turned down an extension to his contract in January during his third season in North Yorkshire. He said, 'After training before the Salisbury game, Colin had a word and told me I was leaving. I had been half-expecting it and when I was driving out of KitKat Crescent and looking back, it was emotional. There are mixed emotions but it was time for a change.' Panther went on to sign for League Two side Exeter.

McEwan collects his belongings from Bootham Crescent following his dismissal. (Nigel Holland)

York supporters put on an impressive flag display for their 2008 FA Trophy semi-final second-leg clash with Torquay at Bootham Crescent. (Garry Atkinson)

A banner spans the length of the David Longhurst Stand for the deciding Trophy semi-final match with Torquay. (David Harrison)

Their hands might be up but Torquay are in no mood to surrender as Richard Brodie attempts to turn the tide in the FA Trophy tie. (David Harrison)

Onome Sodje calls for a foul against Torquay in the FA Trophy semi-final home clash. The club would later appeal successfully against his deportation, only for Sodje to leave for Barnsley. (Ally Carmichael)

Manny Panther bids farewell to York City fans after his last home match against Farsley Celtic. (Anthony Chappel-Ross)

5

'THEY'RE NOT GOOD ENOUGH, ARE THEY?'

Colin Walker will look back on the summer of 2008 having learned one painful lesson: Gretna might be the destination of choice for eloping couples planning a shotgun marriage, but the small border town is no place to visit if you are a professional football manager looking to rebuild your midfield engine room. Rookie trio Ben Wilkinson, Steven Hogg and Niall Henderson were all recruited having previously plied their trade at the bankrupted Scottish Premier League club. All three would also flop as Walker's short managerial reign unravelled.

Walker's transfer market business started encouragingly when 'keeper Michael Ingham returned to the club following a loan spell from Sunderland five years earlier. A past Northern Ireland international, Ingham had once conceded a goal from Lukas Podolski in a friendly against Germany. Experienced Burton utility man Mark Greaves was also signed up and made club captain. But, despite being under contract with the Minstermen for another year, promising midfielder Nicky Wroe was put on the transfer list after claims were made that he no longer wanted to play for the club. He subsequently joined Torquay for a modest five-figure sum.

Off the pitch, the City of York Council agreed to take over the club's onerous annual £138,000 Football Foundation loan repayments, with staffing matters and urgency committee chair Steve Galloway explaining, 'We have an opportunity to help sport in York – more particularly, the football club is an asset to the city and they need to be able to see a way forward.' Galloway later revealed that land behind York Racecourse, known as Bustardthorpe, was the latest area to be considered as a possible site for a new community sports stadium.

Martyn Woolford, meanwhile, returned from a Caribbean trip with England C to comment on growing speculation regarding his future, pointing out, 'I've always said I wouldn't leave York for another Conference club. I would be setting my sights higher and probably higher than League Two as well to be honest, but you have to wait and see. I've not heard anything and my sights are fully set on York City.' Australian striker Daniel McBreen rejoined the club soon afterwards, following the previous season's loan spell, after being released by St Johnstone. City fans also raised the £10,000 funding shortfall to keep the youth team in existence with television commentator Jon Champion – a fan of the Minstermen – donating the largest individual sum of £1,000.

Having completed pre-season, Walker claimed his team were one of ten capable of mounting a promotion challenge. But star man Woolford left to join League One Scunthorpe for an undisclosed six-figure sum the day before the campaign kicked off. The highly rated, twenty-two-year-old winger had turned down an improved contract two months earlier and the club did not want to run the risk of losing him for a tribunal-fixed fee the following summer. On Woolford's departure, Walker said, 'He's going to better his career and it gives us a bit of time to replace him and get on with our season, hoping to get promoted. I've got to make my squad hopefully as good as it was with Martyn in it.' With that in mind, Walker added Simon Russell and Gavin Rothery to his squad, while Peter Bore and Peter Holmes were brought in on loan.

Initial signs were encouraging, when Walker's team started the season with back-to-back 1-0 wins against Crawley and Wrexham. The previous season's team had only kept back-to-back clean sheets once but the class of 2008/09 went on to draw each of their next five matches. The last game in that sequence saw Billy McEwan's new Mansfield team draw 1-1 at Bootham Crescent. McEwan was applauded on to the pitch by fans from all four sides of the ground and, with the two teams pitted against each other in the FA Cup and Setanta Shield, he tackled his old side four times before early November.

The Minstermen extended their unbeaten start to the season with a 2-0 home win over Woking following a Danny Bunce own goal and McBreen's first-half strike and, as a result, Walker equalled another club record, belonging to Denis Smith, who also kicked off the 1984/85 campaign undefeated in his first eight games. At the time, next opponents Kettering were the only other undefeated Blue Square Bet Premier side. The Poppies promptly become the last remaining unbeaten side after walloping Walker's men 4-2 at their Rockingham Road home, and the defeat heralded the start of a six-match sequence without a win. During that time, a 1-1 home draw with Salisbury saw City fail to muster a single shot until the forty-second minute, with the team becoming increasingly dull to watch and bereft of attacking fluency.

A 0-0 home draw with Cambridge also witnessed the visitors manage just one shot all game, while their hosts only forced one save in a drab ninety minutes. Set-pieces remained the team's biggest goal threat and Walker attempted to improve attacking matters by making unsuccessful inquiries for ex-York striker Clayton Donaldson, Kidderminster forward Justin Richards and Stevenage's Iyseden Christie.

Following a run of one win in twelve matches, the Minstermen eventually managed a 2-0 triumph at Woking with Wilkinson and McBreen on target. Another 2-0 triumph against Rushden and a 0-0 FA Cup fourth qualifying round draw against Mansfield also meant the team were, at least, still unbeaten at Bootham Crescent nine home matches into the season. In between, twenty-one-year-old striker Brodie, called up by the England C selectors a month earlier, was farmed out on loan to Barrow. City then went out of the FA Cup with a whimper in their replay at Mansfield, managing just one shot on target at Field Mill – a statistic that was becoming worryingly commonplace and was repeated in the next game – another 1-0 defeat at Oxford.

After the Mansfield match, Walker was harangued by a section of the visitors' support and responded, 'I think the fans pay their money and they are entitled to chant what they want. I have confidence in myself and I have confidence in my players. Come the end of the season, I don't think we will be far away.' The manager's long search for a new striker finally ended with the capture of thirty-three-year-old Bruce Dyer. The former Premier League star, who became the first million-pound teenager when he moved from Watford to Crystal Palace in 1994, was handed a two-month contract but arrived having failed to net a senior goal in twenty-one months – a period encompassing eighteen matches. He also joined City having played no football in 2008/09.

The unbeaten home record subsequently came to an end following a 2-1 defeat to Torquay, with the visitors grabbing a dubious ninetieth minute winner when Ingham appeared to be fouled. Another 1-0 loss at Cambridge United was decided by a bizarre Ben Purkiss own goal when the right-back beat Ingham with a misplaced chested back-pass. Walker departed three days later with his team having failed to score a goal from open play in six matches. Only Greaves had troubled the scoresheet twice during that period with headers from corners while Brodie was hitting the net on a consistent basis for Barrow, scoring four times in seven outings. Throwing David McGurk upfield as an emergency striker in the closing stages at the Abbey Stadium proved to be Walker's final throw of the dice as manager. In the aftermath of the defeat but prior to his dismissal, Walker admitted, 'I can't defend anybody. I tried to change shape to get them all going, but it was quite difficult. I think it's only the second time this season that I can say it was a poor team performance and the other team were better than us. I'm big enough to say that and the players have got to pick themselves up for a tough game against Crawley on Sunday.'

Walker was relieved of his duties having won just three of his last seventeen fixtures and with the side fifteenth in the table.

Explaining the decision, communications director Sophie Hicks (*neé* McGill) said, 'We don't feel that enough progress has been made over the last twelve months and we are a club that has ambitions and, ideally, want to be in a play-off position. We have made the change as we feel we need to try and improve so we have a chance of success at the end of the season.' Walker's reign, therefore, ended just one year and five days after it had begun. Having initially declined to comment on his dismissal, the following week he defended his record at the helm, which included two more victories than defeats. City also claimed the same number of draws – sixteen as wins under his stewardship, however.

'If you put my record down on paper, I'm well aware that we had too many draws but it wasn't too bad,' Walker reasoned. 'We all understand what football's like though and I think the football club are still ambitious enough to think they will get promoted.'

Walker's downfall was perhaps best explained by the quality of his signings. Adequate replacements were never found for the likes of Woolford, Wroe and Manny Panther, while Ingham was arguably the sole success from the eighteen players he recruited permanently and on loan during his period at the Bootham Cresent helm.

Walker's assistant Eric Winstanley was also sacked, which left youth-team manager Neil Redfearn in temporary charge for the next match at home to Crawley. Redfearn fielded the side he claimed Walker would have selected, with two teenagers on the left side of his 4-4-2 formations in Andy McWilliams and Liam Shepherd. McWilliams, though, conceded a last-minute penalty that led to the visitors snatching a point from a 2-2 draw. Former Port Vale manager Martin Foyle was subsequently installed as the new boss for the next match at his hometown Salisbury with Redfearn named as his assistant.

Foyle had been working as a coach at Conference rivals Wrexham under Brian Little and, on his appointment, chairman Jason McGill said, 'Martin has a very impressive CV and, importantly for us, has an extremely good knowledge of Conference football and what is required to succeed in this division. He also has the very best coaching qualifications and, having been a great centre-forward himself, we believe he will help our own strikers to develop and grow.' Foyle was approached by the club having been earmarked as an 'outstanding candidate' twelve months earlier, when his CV landed on the club's desk following McEwan's dismissal.

Despite the team hovering just five points above the relegation zone, Foyle took over, signalling his intention to gatecrash the play-off places, saying, 'If we can put a run together and I'm looking at within weeks, rather than the next two or three months, then confidence will grow and the play-offs will easily be within our grasp.' On his footballing philosophy, Foyle added, 'I'm here to play attractive football when it's right and score goals. Looking at the defence, it's quite mean so, hopefully, we can break down the forward play a bit and make things simpler.'

City's 1993 Wembley play-off final hero Jon McCarthy gave his former Port Vale teammate a ringing endorsement, saying, 'He is a genuine bloke, who is full of enthusiasm for the game and has a very broad knowledge of football. He always wants to play the game the right way. Provided he gets the right resources and backing, I am certain he will do a great job.' He also pointed to Foyle's proven record of improving strikers, citing Billy Paynter, Akpo Sodje and Leon Constantine as examples of frontmen who did well for Vale before moving on to bigger clubs for sizeable transfer fees.

Another York legend and former Vale teammate Keith Houchen echoed McCarthy's sentiments, saying, 'What's riled me watching York this season is that they've been doing all the hard work and got on top in games but then, despite getting in some fantastic areas, they've looked like they've not been shown how to score goals. It's been letting the rest of the team down and the first thing I thought when I heard about Martin coming to York is that he will rectify that straight away. He will show them the right ways to score and see if they can do it and, if they can't, he'll bring new strikers in.

'Foyley himself was as good a finisher as I ever played with. If he was one on one with a 'keeper, you would be walking back to the halfway line for the restart. That hasn't been the case at York for a while and he will show the forwards a lot of different ways to score that had never entered their minds before.'

Foyle made his first signing on the eve of the Salisbury match when he brought Gainsborough Trinity winger Adam Smith to the club.

After an Ingham howler gave the hosts a first-half lead at Salisbury through Charlie Griffin, Brodie grabbed an eighty-third-minute equaliser off the bench after being recalled from his loan spell with Barrow. Afterwards, Brodie admitted he was already benefiting from Foyle's striking tips, saying, 'I've learned bits and bobs off him already and I am thoroughly looking forward to working with him.'

The measure of the task faced by Foyle, however, was outlined in the next match as a Grays team that had lost their last ten away games left Bootham Crescent with a 1-0 win. City were booed off, while one Grays supporter chose to celebrate the end of his team's losing streak in the most literal sense with only a strategically-placed sock to spare his blushes. At the final whistle, the new manager conceded, 'There are more problems here than I probably anticipated. The team has only won three of the last twenty-three matches so things can't have been that good, but confidence is a lot lower than I thought from speaking to the players and watching them in training.'

A 1-1 draw at a Histon side that had won their last eight games thanks to another Brodie goal though hinted at an improvement, and was followed up by back-to-back wins against Northwich in the FA Trophy and at home to Ebbsfleet, who were seen off 3-1. Brodie bagged a brace against Northwich and, prior to the Trophy tie, Foyle challenged his squad to reach Wembley in the competition. He said, 'The fact that the players have been close to Wembley before will be brought up and I will ask them how much further they want to go. There has been doom and gloom around this place for a number of years now so it would be great to put a smile on people's faces, but there's a lot of hard work to be done to get there between now and then.'

Brodie was on target again against the Fleet, extending his record of scoring in every game he had played under Foyle to a fourth match. Dyer, meanwhile, retired from the game with back and hamstring problems. A fifth own goal of the season though, scored by Greaves, following previous blunders by McGurk, Mark Robinson, Purkiss and Daniel Parslow, resulted in a 2-1 Boxing Day defeat at Burton.

The own goals had cost City a staggering eight points, meaning the difference between the club's then sixteenth-placed standing and a position just outside the play-off places. Instead, a 2-1 home defeat against Altrincham saw the club end 2008 sitting just four points above the Blue Square Bet Premier drop zone, with seven of the eight teams below them boasting two games in hand. Foyle promised to weed out the 'weak-hearted' members of his squad afterwards, but the manager's New Year's resolution to lift the doom and gloom at the club did not get off to the best of starts with a 3-1 home defeat to Burton on 1 January.

The Trophy continued to offer some respite, with a surprise 2-1 win at Oxford courtesy of goals from McBreen and Brodie – his fifteenth of the campaign. By then, Foyle's former teammate at Port Vale Andy Porter had been brought in as his new number two following Redfearn's departure for a youth-team role at Leeds United. Foyle also signed a raft of out-of-favour Wrexham players during the January transfer window, with Kyle Critchell, Christian Smith, Simon Brown and Levi Mackin all arriving in North Yorkshire. Another former Wrexham man, Shaun Pejic, joined them the following month.

The club went on to announce worrying losses of £413,000 for the year ending June 2008. It was revealed that wage salaries had swollen to a total of just under £855,000, which represented 74 per cent of the club's turnover. On the annual accounts, finance director Terry Doyle said, 'What has become evident is that our income cannot, on its own, sustain the Football League structure we have tried to maintain at the club and produce a team which can compete effectively in the Conference. We continue to look at all aspects of the club to identify where savings can be made, but the reality is that without JM Packaging's support the club would be in a difficult trading position. It is likely we will continue to require further funding from JM Packaging this year.'

Back on the pitch, Brodie grabbed another two goals in a 3-0 win over a poor Lewes team, taking his tally to ten in as many matches under Foyle. Teenager Adam Boyes then scored in only his second start to give City a first-half lead in their third-round Trophy tie at Kidderminster. Martin Brittain's seventy-fifth-minute equaliser forced a replay, which was won by the Minstermen following an extraordinary penalty shoot-out. All twenty-two players left on the pitch at the end of extra time converted from the spot, including teenage debutant Josh Radcliffe. Robinson and Rusk then netted again for the Minstermen, as did Kidderminster's Darryl Knights in between, before Ingham saved from Justin Richards to end a marathon evening. Earlier, Richards had cancelled out McBreen's seventy-fourth-minute opening goal and the score remained 1-1 after two hours of play. A superstitious Foyle refused to watch any of the twenty-six penalties. The FA later confirmed that no two teams had ever converted the first twenty-five spot-kicks during a professional penalty shoot-out in England. McBreen, in his first game since news broke from Australia that he intended to return home to play for North Queensland Fury at the end of the season, then got both goals in a 2-0 home win as City reached the semi-finals of the Trophy at the expense of Havant & Waterlooville.

The Minstermen's league form remained a concern though, as a crisis-torn Weymouth team, who had been beaten 9-0 by Rushden the game before, almost earned a share of the spoils in a dire encounter at Bootham Crescent, despite fielding five players under the age of eighteen. Brodie only made maximum points certain in the ninetieth minute with his second header of the match, but his understandable exuberance at scoring his twentieth goal of the season was shared by few home fans. The team took a big step towards emulating past heroes such as Dean Kiely, Paul Barnes and Wayne Hall, however, by becoming only the second City side to play at Wembley when goals from Simon Rusk and Purkiss sealed a 2-0 Trophy semi-final first-leg win at Telford.

For the first and final time, Foyle, normally a big advocate of a flat back four, employed a 3-5-2 formation that arguably best suited a squad with a surplus of competent centre halves, few natural wide men and forward-thinking full-backs in Purkiss and Robinson. Party poppers were then handed out in the directors' box and fans invaded the pitch as City completed a 4-1 aggregate semi-final Trophy victory over Telford at Bootham Crescent. Brodie and McBreen scored for City with Andy Brown's late consolation counting for nothing. Archbishop of York Dr John Sentamu joined in raucous celebrations as players, management and board members jumped up and down in the directors' box in front of jubilant City supporters.

Afterwards, Foyle talked of the importance of making Wembley a springboard for better fortunes in the league, saying, 'I think getting the players focussed for the rest of the season would have been harder had we gone out of the Trophy. It's not a slight on our players, because it would be the same at any club, but I will be surprised if any of them are in the treatment room between now and the end of the season. The competition for places between now and then will ensure that Wembley isn't a distraction.'

On the implications of reaching Wembley for only the second time in the club's history, Foyle added, 'I probably didn't realise what it means to the people who work within the club but there's been a few crying who have seen the good times, but more bad times. I'm absolutely delighted we have delivered for them. Hopefully the victory can pull everybody together because, since I've been here, it's felt like a bit of a divided camp. There's still a lot of work to be done though.'

An emotional Sophie Hicks added, 'The last six to eight years have been difficult ones for the club and our supporters have been amazing, so we hope 9 May will be a reward for all the hard work they have put in.'

But league results showed little sign of an upturn, and a dismal 1-0 defeat at Grays in the first game of the final month of the season saw the Minstermen drop into the relegation zone with seven games to play. Rusk was also sent off for a petulant injury-time kick at home captain Stuart Thurgood. Directors, management and players shared heated views in the changing rooms afterwards, where a few home truths were aired. Foyle was livid with Rusk, fuming, 'I would like to see him snapping at people earlier in the game, when we have been ducking out of tackles, instead of having a go at them on the floor'. City subsequently went a fifth game without scoring as Sodje saw his first-half penalty saved during a 0-0 home draw with Oxford.

A desperate 2-1 home defeat to Northwich followed and then another goalless stalemate with Barrow meant York had won just three of their last twenty-six league games. Those victories had also been against lowly trio Ebbsfleet, Lewes and Weymouth. Offering a rhetorical question after the Northwich match, Foyle pointed out, 'They're not good enough, are they?' After the Barrow game, though, Foyle claimed the club boasted 'promotion material' following a seventeenth clean sheet of the season. His statement did not refer to success in the division below either. He believed the team's goalkeeper Ingham, the defence and a midfield pairing of Christian Smith and Mackin could provide a strong enough spine to challenge at the other end of their current division. 'In the defence and the midfield, we have a good platform. I believe they are promotion material,' Foyle reasoned. It was a favourable run-in, though, that ultimately ensured safety for the Minstermen.

McBreen ended his terrible twenty-one hour and forty-six minute wait for a league goal by securing a 1-0 home win over Eastbourne, meaning the team climbed out of the bottom four going into the final week of the season. There had been high hopes for McBreen when he had signed for the club in the summer, but his season, aside from selective Trophy highlights, had been more a story of Desperate Dan than Supermac.

A 2-1 home win over Forest Green, thanks to Boyes and a Terry Burton own goal, on the last Tuesday night of the season then left the team needing just one point to stay up ahead of their penultimate match of the season at another relegation-threatened team Weymouth three days later. City went on to win 2-1 on the South Coast, but not without big scares along the way. After Brodie's twenty-third goal of the season, Cliff Akurang levelled for the hosts following an Ingham mistake. Weymouth then searched for the winning goal that would have heaped on the pressure ahead of the Minstermen's final match at Lewes two days later. McGurk was forced into a goal-line clearance, before it was left to eighteen-year-old Boyes to preserve City's Blue Square Bet Premier status in the seventy-seventh minute. Foyle was in little mood for celebration at the final whistle, admitting that 'it wasn't a great performance'.

Despite Wembley places still being up for grabs, City then showed little stomach for the Lewes game, drawing 1-1 at a team, including five teenagers, whose relegation had been confirmed back in March. Youth-team coach Steve Torpey was given his full City debut at the age of thirty-eight, with Foyle even considering him for Trophy final action. Skipper Parslow was also rested for the game against his wishes, denying him the chance to have played in every minute of the campaign. The team finished the season seventeenth, matching the lowest position in the club's history, set during that first Conference campaign in 2004/05.

But a final safety margin of eight points flattered a side who were entrenched in the bottom four just ten days earlier, and only ensured safety in a shaky penultimate match of the season. With a fair degree of understatement, Foyle's final comment on the 2008/09 league campaign was 'we've got to be a lot better and need some fresh faces in to liven the place up'. City's board pledged to provide better fortunes with a club statement, reading 'over the coming weeks the board will be preparing budgets for next season. We are determined to achieve success in the league and we will be giving our management team the best possible budget we can to try to achieve this'.

A total of 11,000 City supporters, more than had attended the club's 1993 League Two play-off final, travelled to Wembley to witness their team get beaten 2-0 by a Stevenage side still recovering from the disappointment of a play-off semi-final defeat. Boyes fired straight at Stevenage 'keeper Chris Day with a decent chance in the first half, and Greaves also blazed another opportunity over; those misses proved as costly as the national stadium's meat and potato pies. Future Wales international and Premier League striker Steve Morison made up for squandering two earlier openings on sixty-eight minutes, when centre-back Mark Roberts headed towards goal from an Andy Drury corner. Morison then poked the ball forward and, when Parslow misjudged his sliding challenge and Purkiss was slow to react, the former Northampton striker seized a second invitation to prod in from 2 yards.

In injury time, Lee Boylan then profited from schoolboy defending after Parslow cleared the ball into touch on the left wing, but then neglected to mark Boylan from the subsequent quick throw-in. The grateful, former West Ham trainee was sent clear on goal by Morison and beat Ingham with a well-executed dipping 12-yard volley.

Foyle lamented afterwards, 'I think the game showed the gulf between Stevenage and ourselves. People still consider York a Football League outfit but there's a big divide.' On his future at the club, he added, 'There's no question about me wanting to be here. There's a big job to be done but, hopefully, I can do something about it in the summer and start with a lot of fresh faces. That would make my job easier because they would be my own players and you live and die by your own decisions, whereas I did not have the money to be explosive in the transfer market when I came in.'

Captain Parslow spelled out his hopes for the future at the final whistle, saying, 'Going forward, I believe that being hard to beat and organised counts for a lot in this league, and I thought we were both of those towards the end of the season. That's something to build on and the manager will reflect on where he needs to strengthen. I'm sure there will be some new faces next season.

'Being in a relegation battle isn't nice. York City should be at the opposite end of the table and that's where we'll hopefully aim to be next season.'

It was clear that Foyle's summer recruits would need to be stronger than those made a year earlier by his predecessor. Russell's recruitment as a replacement for Woolford proved woefully inadequate, with the ex-Kidderminster man managing just one goal – a wind-assisted fluke direct from a corner at Barrow – and one assist in thirty-three underwhelming outings.

While City's strikers also came in for criticism during the 2008/09 season, the standard of service they received would have made Basil Fawlty blush, as right-back Purkiss finished the campaign with the most goal assists. The season also ended on a sour note for Purkiss' fellow full-back Robinson. Robinson was released and admitted that the memories of his two-year spell with the Minstermen would be forever tarnished by Foyle's decision to leave him on the bench for the FA Trophy final, after he had been one of only three players to play every previous minute in the competition. He had even been used to model and advertise the purple shirt that was used in the final, before centre-half Pejic was preferred to play instead of him at left back under Wembley's famous arch. Commenting on his treatment, Robinson said, 'I got a phone call from the chairman about promoting the shirt and he said I was one of the longest-serving players and congratulated me on how I'd been doing over the past few months. He told me he could think of nobody better to promote the shirt. To be then left out at Wembley tarnished the whole thing.'

Robinson also felt that selling Woolford on the eve of the new season proved detrimental to the team's efforts. 'We won our first two games and drew the next six,' he added. 'Well, Woolly could have won all those games for us.'

Billy McEwan returns to Bootham Crescent with his Mansfield team and shakes hands with his successor and former assistant Colin Walker. (Ally Carmichael)

Martin Foyle is unveiled as manager with (from left to right) Sophie Hicks, Jason McGill, Neil Redfearn and Rob McGill. (Mike Tipping)

Steve Morison opens the scoring for Stevenage in their 2-0 FA Trophy win. (Nigel Holland)

Dispirited City players Richard Brodie, Shaun Pejic, Michael Ingham, David McGurk, Daniel Parslow (partially hidden) and Levi Mackin head back for the restart after Morison's goal. (Nigel Holland)

6

'I'M GOING TO LOCK MYSELF IN A ROOM'

Possibly the biggest legacy of York City's disappointing FA Trophy final defeat was that the funds generated from the match allowed Martin Foyle to replace large chunks of the underperforming squad that had got the club to Wembley. A total of nine players followed homeward-bound Daniel McBreen and Mark Robinson out of the exit door, including the likes of Simon Rusk, Mark Greaves and Ben Wilkinson.

Midfielder Andy Ferrell and left-winger Craig Nelthorpe, meanwhile, became the first new arrivals from Kidderminster and Oxford respectively. Striker Richard Pacquette and left-back James Meredith were the next to be signed from Maidenhead and Shrewsbury respectively while a £10,000 bid for Ebbsfleet defender Darius Charles was rejected after the offer was voted on by the Kent outfit's MyFootballClub internet owners. A total of 1,977 were against accepting the transfer with just sixty-six in favour.

Striker Michael Rankine was captured though in a £10,000 deal from Rushden & Diamonds, while Onome Sodje – City's twenty-year-old striker – walked out on the club to sign for Championship club Barnsley. It came to light that the Minstermen would not be entitled to a transfer fee for his services either, as Sodje had been playing for the club on a non-contract basis due to his lack of a work permit. During that time, City officials had successfully campaigned against his deportation to Nigeria but, after that matter was resolved on his behalf, Sodje decided to head for Oakwell rather than sign a contract extension at Bootham Crescent. Permanent residency in the UK was not normally granted to immigrant players outside the Football League, but Sodje's appeal to the Home Office had been finally accepted in April. The Archbishop of York, Dr John Sentamu, and York MP Hugh Bayley had also been enlisted for their support, but the player, who had been a regular on the bench under Foyle, left the club having scored twenty-four goals in a hundred outings.

Midfielder Alex Lawless arrived from Forest Green shortly afterwards, and the club went on to announce the £80,000 capture of Ebbsfleet trio Charles, Neil Barrett and Michael Gash. Centre-back Charles later decided against a move to Bootham Crescent, though, because he wanted to remain in London so Mansfield defender Alan O'Hare was recruited instead. Barrett still signed and, after another centre-back Djoumin Sangare was brought in, Gash eventually completed a £55,000 move following another MyFootballClub vote. On Foyle's summer recruitment drive, communications director Sophie Hicks said, 'We have given Martin Foyle the best possible resources to put together a team that will deliver success for our supporters in the coming season. The focus for us has to be the first team. That solves all our issues – if we were to gain promotion. As a board, we felt very confident with the way he presented his plans for the coming season and we have given him maximum support. It is fair to say this is the most support we have ever given to a manager.'

Some of the money spent on the new signings was also recouped when Adam Boyes joined Scunthorpe.

On the eve of the new campaign, parents of City's under-eighteen scholars, meanwhile, were asked to raise an annual £19,000 shortfall in funding to preserve the future of a youth team that in the past had nurtured the emerging talents of Boyes as well as high-profile trio Jonathan Greening, Graeme Murty and Richard Cresswell. At an extraordinary meeting with first-year apprentices' families, chairman Jason McGill announced initially that £57,000 a year would need to be found, but pledges from his company JM Packaging, club sponsors CLP and the Supporters' Trust eventually reduced that onus.

As the new season approached, following bottom-half finishes in successive Blue Square Bet Premier campaigns, optimism was high for better fortunes in 2009/10. But that enthusiasm was dampened somewhat by a mixed bag of pre-season results, which culminated in a 3-1 defeat to AFC Halifax Town – who were plying their trade three divisions below the Minstermen at the time. New signing Nelthorpe was sent off for landing an elbow on ex-York defender Mark Hotte in the match and Foyle slammed the player afterwards, saying, 'Craig Nelthorpe led with his arm and, rightly so, he was sent off. I won't protect him because I can't.' The fiery left winger's fledgling City career then took another turn for the worse when he was arrested, along with teammates Rankine, Gash and Michael Ingham, after an altercation in a sandwich shop during a night out in York after the match. Foyle decided to leave the matter in the hands of the relevant authorities rather than dishing out any internal punishment, saying, 'I want to make it clear that I gave these boys permission to go out, the whole squad went out. They all had a bite to eat together and it was their night to let their hair down after working really hard during the pre-season. Typically, at the end of the night there was an incident. It's hard to comment, as I haven't got all the facts. It is all on CCTV so I'm going to wait to see what that brings to light. I've had players in trouble before, it happens, but I'm taking no immediate action until I know more.'

Prior to the new season, it was announced that the deal that gave Nestlé stadium-naming rights would end in January, meaning KitKat Crescent could revert back to its more-recognised Bootham Crescent moniker to the delight of club traditionalists.

In the opening game of the season at highly fancied Oxford, Ingham was only required to make one save prior to the eighty-eighth minute when his team were leading 1-0 thanks to Richard Brodie's first-half effort. But Matt Green then capitalised on a Daniel Parslow mistake to level the scores with two minutes of normal time remaining. Then, in the first minute of stoppage time, Ingham failed to punch cleanly amid a crowded penalty box and centre-back Mark Creighton side-footed into an empty net. It was a cruel end to a promising performance that had lifted spirits after the Halifax debacle and subsequent off-pitch shenanigans.

City went on to record a first win in their third match with a 2-0 home defeat of Forest Green courtesy of Rankine's penalty and an Adam Smith effort. But a defeat at Wrexham, followed by a point at Hayes and Yeading United, rescued by substitute Pacquette's eighty-third-minute equaliser, left Foyle's team with just that one victory from their opening five games. A potential crossroads for City's season was then provided at Gateshead where, with the score deadlocked at 1-1 thanks to a Brodie equaliser, Pacquette was sent off for retaliation on fifty-six minutes. The ten men displayed a steely spirit, however, that would go on to characterise their campaign with Gash heading in the winning goal from a brilliant Ferrell cross ten minutes from time.

Back-to-back home wins over Histon (3-1) – a bogey side that City had never managed to beat previously – and Crawley (2-0) followed and Foyle's team were up and running, clocking up a hat-trick of consecutive home wins for the first time in three-and-a-half years. The level of progress made in just five months was then illustrated in a 1-1 home draw against FA Trophy final tormentors Stevenage. Sangare's stoppage-time header earned City a share of the spoils, leaving Foyle to hail his players' 'Yorkshire grit', even though the goal-scorer hailed from France and the team also contained a pair of Welshmen, two Geordies, an Irishman and an Aussie! A 3-2 win at Tamworth, secured by Ferrell, Brodie and Sangare goals, saw City go ten games unbeaten.

That run ended following an unlucky 1-0 loss at Salisbury, but leaders Oxford were then fortunate to leave Bootham Crescent with a 1-1 draw after Simon Clist scored with the visitors' only on-target attempt of the afternoon on eighty-one minutes. Rankine had earlier opened the scoring for the hosts, who also finished the game strongly despite a red card for Meredith. City went on to claim a 1-1 draw at promotion favourites Luton with Barrett giving the visitors a first-half lead. Soon afterwards, centre-back Luke Graham arrived on loan from Mansfield with Chris Carruthers having also been recruited from Oxford on the same basis.

In the FA Cup, meanwhile, first-half goals from emerging strike partners Rankine and Brodie secured a comfortable 2-0 home win over a part-time Bedworth team, for whom future York hero Matty Blair lined up on the wing. Brodie then bagged a brace as League Two Crewe were dumped out at the next stage during a thrilling 3-2 first-round proper home win. His second goal, on eighty-seven minutes, was worthy of winning any cup tie, as he started and finished off a move that saw him burst powerfully into the penalty box and repel challenges from three defenders before lifting the ball over Crewe 'keeper Steve Phillips. Substitute Pacquette had only equalised two minutes earlier with his first touch during a grandstand finish to the match. The prolific Brodie went on to claim his first City hat-trick in a 3-2 home win over Chester, although the result was later wiped from the history books after the visitors failed to complete their Blue Square Bet Premier campaign due to financial troubles. City ended November with a 100 per cent record of six wins, earning Foyle and Brodie the Blue Square Bet Premier's Manager and Player of the Month awards respectively.

The month ended with a 2-1 FA Cup win at Cambridge that saw the Minstermen reach the magical third round of the competition for the first time in eight years. Rankine opened the scoring with a fantastic 25-yard strike at the Abbey Stadium and Brodie also converted from the penalty spot, meaning Anthony Tonkin's late effort proved merely a consolation. A 2-1 win at Wrexham, courtesy of Carruthers' first City goal and Brodie's twentieth of the season, then meant the team equalled a club record of eight straight victories. That tally sat alongside the previous longest winning streak set in 1955 by the famous Happy Wanderers' FA Cup semi-final team. Uniquely, each of the victories had been secured by a one-goal margin, proving the Minstermen could doggedly defend slender leads under Foyle, as well as play the expansive football that typified some of their early-season performances. Brodie also became the first City player to reach twenty goals in a season by the first weekend in December. Indeed, only 1955 legend Arthur Bottom and Paul Aimson had ever reached that landmark before the turn of a calendar year.

Off the pitch, the Minstermen announced a modest profit of £30,000 for the year ending June 2009, largely due to the sale of Martyn Woolford and the FA Trophy final appearance. It was the first time the club had made a profit since 2004 – the year the club were relegated from the Football League. Finance director Terry Doyle still issued a word of warning, though, saying, 'We have still only made a small profit during what many clubs would consider a successful season by reaching Wembley. To run a competitive Blue Square Premier club on our basic level of income, you are going to incur losses of between £350,000 and £400,000.'

Foyle's side failed to set an outright club record for consecutive wins when they drew 0-0 at FA Trophy first round hosts Hinckley United, in a match that saw neither side manage a shot on target until the seventy-fifth minute. Another Brodie hat-trick, though, dispatched the Leicestershire part-timers in a 3-1 replay win at Bootham Crescent. City then ended the year in style by beating Mansfield at home 3-0 with Brodie claiming his twenty-fourth and twenty-fifth goals of the season.

The Minstermen kicked off 2011 with an FA Cup third-round tie at Stoke City, who included £23 million worth of talent in their side, including seven full internationals. It was a one-time Sunderland misfit who cost nothing, though, that proved the difference between the Premier League outfit and their non-League opponents. Rory Delap's famous long throws were the undoing of Foyle's team after Barrett had gloriously headed City in front midway through the first half from a Lawless free-kick. Prior to the game, 'keeper Ingham had said, 'They are all 6 foot 2 inches or 6 foot 3 inches, but we've dealt with that for the last eighteen months. Nobody has overpowered us at set plays. I have got every faith in my back four.' Afterwards, though, the shocked City 'keeper confessed that Delap's throw-ins were more troublesome than expected: 'To be quite honest, they were ridiculous,' he said. 'You watch them on TV and they look bad on that, but it was worse out there. I wouldn't like to play against that every week. It's hard for a goalkeeper because he throws it flat and fast. You can't attack it in case someone nips in front of you.'

Home boss Tony Pulis was very complimentary afterwards, though, paying special tribute to the 4,000 travelling army of away fans, saying, 'You have to give huge credit to York as a club because to bring so many supporters here was fantastic. The players also did them proud by working very hard.' Many City supporters had arrived at the Britannia Stadium late, with the game's kick-off delayed as players and supporters struggled to negotiate snowy conditions on the M62 and M6. They were sent delirious by Barrett's first-half goal. But, within two minutes, Parslow had sliced a Delap throw into the roof of his own net and, seconds later, Ricardo Fuller got a scrambled second for the hosts from the same source. Matthew Etherington then settled the tie just before the hour mark with a curling free-kick. A 4-1 home victory over Hayes & Yeading, courtesy of Carruthers, another two-goal Brodie blast and Kevin Gall, subsequently set a new club record of eight consecutive league wins.

The FA Trophy home tie against Corby, won 1-0 by City, later provided a poignant moment to mark the twentieth anniversary of David Longhurst's death from a heart attack on the Bootham Crescent pitch. Corby was Longhurst's hometown club and supporters from both clubs laid wreaths in front of the David Longhurst Stand before the match, placing football firmly into perspective.

The Minstermen extended their league record to a ninth win on the trot by winning 1-0 at Cambridge after Barrett's third goal of the season; but the sequence ended with a 1-1 away draw against Histon where Ben Purkiss' twentieth-minute goal was cancelled out in the second half by Bradley Hudson-Odoi. When Rankine secured a 1-0 win at Kettering in early February, however, the Minstermen had moved within a point of long-time front-runners Oxford and Stevenage. A cautious Foyle was quick to play down his side's title chances, though, saying, 'There might be a big thing made of the other teams dropping points at the weekend but we still have a batch of away games to come. Seven points from our last nine on the road is a fantastic return but we need to play a bit better still.' Indeed, it proved to be the nearest Foyle's team would come to the division's top spot as a run of seven games without a win followed, including a 2-1 FA Trophy quarter-final exit at Barrow, where Jason Walker was on target for the hosts.

The disappointing sequence started with a 1-0 defeat – the club's first in the league for fourteen weeks – at Ebbsfleet during which Brodie was sent off after a collision with home midfielder Dean Pooley left the latter requiring five stitches to a facial injury. Moses Ashikodi scored the only goal of the match while Brodie was banned for the next three games. City fought out a 0-0 home draw with Luton in the next game and then lost for the first time in twenty-four matches at Bootham Crescent, going down 1-0 to Eastbourne. Brodie was clearly being missed, with Rankine and Gash extending their record of never having scored when paired together in attack to a ninth game. Gash, at that point, had netted once in eighteen outings and Rankine once in fifteen. After Barrow in the Trophy, Forest Green then became the third relegation-threatened team to beat City in a week despite Brodie's return, and Salisbury made it four consecutive defeats with a 2-1 triumph at Bootham Crescent.

Off the pitch, meanwhile, it was mooted that Bootham Crescent could be redeveloped as an alternative to moving stadium. The idea, which was dependent on acquiring land from the Ministry of Defence behind the Popular Stand, like many others never reached the drawing board. It took a Courtney Pitt goal at Mansfield to eventually ensure the team returned to winning ways. Brodie, however, saw a penalty saved, meaning he had failed to net for nine games. Kidderminster were seen off in the next match after a solitary Barrett goal, while Jason McGill hit out at continued heel-dragging from the City of York Council on the issue of a new community stadium. He said, 'At present, the messages coming from certain York council leaders are negative and underwhelming. It will not do to palm us off with statements about the economy, hard times for the public purse and the questioning of the financial health of the football club.

'Deloitte have given us a clean bill of health after a recent extensive, forensic accounting investigation so come on City of York Council, make a definite statement of intent towards the new stadium and put smiles back onto the faces of the people you represent. If you cannot make that commitment then, at least, we all know where we stand.

'We can say we have done our best to save York City Football Club. With your hand on your heart, can you say you have done the same? Enough of the talking, delays, false promises and political posturing. It is now time for positive action.'

Cllr Steve Galloway, the council's executive member for city strategy who represented the Liberal Democrats, was quick to respond to McGill's challenge, saying, 'We are continuing to follow the timetable we have agreed with the football club. We would expect the next report to be published in the summer.' But Conservative leader Coun Ian Gillies retorted, 'If Jason McGill wants a commitment of millions of pounds to be spent on York City now, then, as an elected representative, I will have to disappoint him.' Labour leader David Scott went on to clarify his party's position, saying, 'The Labour Group are 100 per cent behind the project. I can understand Jason McGill's frustrations at what seems like slow progress but there is a process to follow.'

Back on the pitch, Tamworth captain Chris Smith earned his team, managed by Gary Mills, a 1-1 away draw at Bootham Crescent. The former York defender followed up to prod home after Ingham had saved the first of the visitors' only two on-target shots of the afternoon from Michael Wylde. Luke Graham had earlier given City the lead. But Foyle's men went on to rattle off three straight wins against Grays (4-0), Altrincham (2-1) and AFC Wimbledon (5-0) to secure a play-off place with four fixtures to spare. Brodie bagged a brace against Grays to end an eleven-game run without a goal and claimed his thirtieth goal of the season with an injury-time match-winning penalty against Alty. He went on to hit a first-half hat-trick in the terrific triumph over Wimbledon, with the match serving as a fitting tribute to 1955 Happy Wanderers legend Sid Storey, who had died during the build-up to the game. His passing was marked by a minute's applause. Rankine also struck twice, justifying his selection ahead of Gash with a man-of-the-match performance that left Foyle in no doubt as to his strongest line-up going into the play-offs – the exact same XI that dispatched the Dons.

The team fulfilled their remaining fixtures with defeats at Eastbourne (3-1) and champions Stevenage (1-0), book-ending home games against Barrow (3-0) and Grays (1-1). The draw with ten-man Grays meant the Minstermen ended the regular season having dropped a disappointing fourteen points against the division's bottom five teams. But that was of little consequence when Brodie's eighty-ninth-minute goal earned his team a 1-0 play-off semi-final, first-leg lead during a tense and evenly matched contest against Luton at Bootham Crescent. The twenty-two-year-old striker burst through on goal after the ball skimmed off Luton centre-back Shane Blackett's head and fired firmly into Mark Tyler's bottom left-hand corner to score his thirty-seventh goal of the season. Foyle kept everybody grounded at the final whistle, however, saying, 'I've told the lads it's only half-time and we know we are in for a hard game at their place. But I'm delighted to have kept a clean sheet against a very good side and to be going there with a lead. There were lots of pluses, but we won't be shouting from the rooftops or getting excited because we are nowhere near there.'

But another 1-0 victory – City's eleventh of the season – at a hostile Kenilworth Road then sent Foyle's team through to a play-off final meeting with Oxford United, who overcame Rushden & Diamonds in the other semi-final. The clean sheet meant the Minstermen had conceded just one goal in their last eleven matches against top-ten opposition. Carruthers scored the only goal of the second leg on forty-seven minutes, pouncing from close range after Tyler could only parry Rankine's firmly struck free-kick. The Hatters' best opportunity came on seventy-seven minutes when Tom Craddock sprinted on to a through ball. An imperious McGurk, however, made up tremendous ground and executed the perfect sliding tackle as the former Middlesbrough trainee prepared to fire past Ingham.

Angry Luton fans spilled on to the pitch at the final whistle, with City's players forced to seek refuge among visiting fans as they were unable to reach the players' tunnel safely. The visiting players and supporters were then pelted with coins. Commenting afterwards, shocked chairman Jason McGill said, 'They were very dreadful scenes. I was very nervous for our supporters and our players. Richard Brodie was hit by a £1 coin and a few other players were hit by missiles. But everyone is safe.' Foyle preferred to comment on football matters, saying, 'We were outstanding and the players deserve credit for the improvements they have made over the last twenty months. We are going to Wembley and I'm looking forward to a great day and a good team to play against.' Long-serving defender McGurk, awarded a rare 10/10 in *The Press* for his second-leg heroics at Luton, admitted there was only one match that counted now. 'It's all right getting to the final but it is not enough,' he pointed out. 'Everything rests on this game. Everything we have been talking about since I have been here. It means everything to the club to get back into the League and hopefully this is the time we are going to do it.'

Oxford's ticket sales outnumbered their opponents roughly four-to-one for the final but Foyle turned that into a positive, arguing, 'That's fine because all the pressure and onus will be on them.' Foyle added that he felt his front two would prove the difference on the day, saying, 'We know they are petrified of Richard Brodie and Michael Rankine.' Oxford hitman James Constable, though, outshone both in the final. The 1988 League Cup winners went in front after fifteen minutes when Ingham was lured off his line by a long punt forward. The former Kidderminster striker beat him to the ball and then hooked it over his shoulder 15 yards from goal. Jack Midson went on to out-jump Meredith, before Matt Green fired over covering defender McGurk into the roof of the net. Six minutes later, Oxford doubled their advantage when the ball smacked Meredith in the face to fortuitously release Constable for a clear run on goal and he made no mistake, driving his 12-yard shot past an exposed Ingham. With City rocking, Midson hit a post but, in the forty-second minute, Foyle's team were handed a lifeline when Purkiss' right-wing cross slipped through Ryan Clarke's fingers and bounced over the line off his nose. Rankine, though, squandered an excellent chance on fifty-four minutes to draw his team level and Barrett, missing his own pre-booked stag do in Las Vegas to play in the final, was also wasteful in front of goal with another opportunity. Foyle later threw on Sangare as an emergency striker but Oxford broke to put the outcome beyond doubt when substitute Alfie Potter beat a helpless Ingham from 10 yards.

At the final whistle, a distraught McGurk said, 'I don't know what I am going to do in the next week. I am going to lock myself in a room, I think. It's just a massive, massive disappointment because I was so confident – not over-confident, just really confident - going into the game. We didn't deal with those two long balls in the first twenty minutes.'

Right-back Purkiss added that the disappointment would take 'weeks to get over' but, after turning down a deal at Bootham Crescent, he went on to join Oxford in the Football League. Ingham, meanwhile, admitted, 'I am beginning to hate this place' after two crushing climaxes to the last two seasons under the world-famous arch. 'I am aiming for automatic promotion next season, not through the play-offs,' he insisted. Oxford chief Chris Wilder reckoned the Minstermen would be a 'real force' in 2010–11 but Foyle signalled a warning, saying, 'People might think it's easy to get over things like this, but it isn't. It will be hard next season.' Pacquette and Nelthorpe were among seven players released after the final. Northampton-based Graham, who had forged a strong defensive backbone with McGurk through the season, also turned down the chance to stay with the Minstermen due to geographical reasons.

Luke Graham kicks off the short-lived celebrations as Neil Barrett briefly gives York the lead at Premier League FA Cup hosts Stoke. (Nigel Holland)

Richard Brodie tries to escape the attentions of Stoke centre-back Robert Huth. (Nigel Holland)

Long-serving defender David McGurk goes close to a rare goal against Eastbourne during the 2009/10 season. (Dave Harrison)

York players mob Chris Carruthers after his play-off semi-final second-leg goal at Luton. (Nigel Holland)

Angry Luton fans confront York supporters in an unsavoury end to the play-off semi-final between the two teams. (Nigel Holland)

York players take cover from thrown coins at Kenilworth Road. (Nigel Holland)

York fans don their Richard Brodie masks prior to the 2010 Blue Square Bet Premier play-off final against Oxford. (Frank Dwyer)

City fans make themselves heard at Wembley in 2010. (Frank Dwyer)

Martin Foyle leads out his team at Wembley to face Oxford. (Nigel Holland)

The 2010 play-off final captain Michael Ingham introduces World Cup winner Geoff Hurst to Martin Foyle. (Nigel Holland)

Oxford goalkeeper Ryan Clarke offers a lifeline when he fumbles Ben Purkiss' cross into the back of his net. (Nigel Holland)

Above left: A tearful Richard Brodie salutes York supporters as his fantastic thirty-seven-goal season ends in play-off agony. (Frank Dwyer)

Above right: Ben Purkiss contemplates defeat at Wembley but, days later, signs for play-off final winners Oxford. (Nigel Holland)

7

'I WANT TO WIN THE TITLE'

With university graduate Ben Purkiss leaving for Oxford to further his football education and Luke Graham homesick, the defensive pair's replacements became key priorities for Martin Foyle in the summer of 2010. With that in mind, Foyle recruited Kidderminster right-back Duane Courtney and Altrincham centre-half Greg Young and later declared, 'Greg has shackled our front two on numerous occasions so I'm absolutely delighted he's decided to join us and Duane has been in my sights for quite a while. He's very much like James Meredith in that he has plenty of pace, energy and can get better.' Foyle failed, however, in a bid to bring Salisbury striker Matt Tubbs to Bootham Crescent. He joined free-spending Crawley instead.

Off the pitch, the club announced that their preferred option for a new stadium site was now at Monks Cross, where the current Huntington Stadium, the council-owned home of Rugby League side York City Knights, would be demolished and a new 6,000-capacity arena erected. Other possible locations, put forward by the City of York Council, involved redeveloping Bootham Crescent, land at Hull Road next to the University of York's Heslington East campus and the Mille Crux and Nestlé North site off Haxby Road. Despite opposing a move to Monks Cross in the past, City chairman Jason McGill argued that the venue was the most achievable, in terms of cost and time frame, with the possibility of adjacent enabling developments to assist funding. McGill added, 'I'm really optimistic about this project and I hope supporters will see it's necessary for the future financial stability of the club and to attract the next generation of supporters'. Foyle went on to add released Walsall winger Peter Till to his squad and signed Forest Green midfielder Jonathan Smith, as well as Braintree forward George Purcell for small undisclosed fees. Goalkeeper David Knight was also recruited on a season-long loan from Histon as cover for Michael Ingham and David McDermott arrived from Kidderminster.

Foyle, though, typically played down his team's prospects for the new campaign, saying, 'People talk about us but there are five or six teams that have bypassed us in terms of spending power and signed one or two players I was after myself. Crawley have blown people out of the water and paid massive signing-on fees, which doesn't occur at York.

'Grimsby have spent unbelievable money as well and have got a big, strong squad, while Darlington, Fleetwood and Newport have also splashed out. It could be hard but I think we are similar to Rushden. We will keep quiet, be in the pack and, hopefully, our team ethic can get us a place in the play-offs again.'

Courtney then proceeded to suffer a nightmare debut for the club on the opening day of the season when he gifted his old team Kidderminster a 2-1 win at Bootham Crescent. Substitute Courtney had only been on the pitch quarter of an hour when he needlessly shoved former teammate Chris McPhee over in the box, and Tom Shaw then dispatched the resulting eighty-ninth-minute penalty. An inglorious start to Courtney's career later saw him try to pick a fight with marksman Michael Rankine and home players were forced to intervene to seemingly prevent the pair from coming to blows. Earlier, Rankine and Richard Brodie had squabbled in unedifying fashion over penalty-taking duties, with the former winning the argument and levelling the scores. On his warring teammates, Foyle said, 'Brodes is on penalties but Ranks came on full of confidence and I don't mind that. It looks a bit petty though when they are arguing with each other and I had a pop about that. At the end of the game, it was handbags really. Sometimes players play with a bit of passion and I wish they'd shown more from the start of the game and during the first forty-five minutes. That type of thing makes me look bad though and I won't condone it. They won't be doing it again. We will keep everything in camp and it's been sorted out in the changing room so there's not a problem.'

On the defeat, Foyle added, 'I'm a bit disappointed but sometimes you need a wake-up call.'

The team slumbered through the first four games, however, before recording their first win – a 3-0 triumph over perennial strugglers Altrincham. Brodie, having suffered a poor start to the season, scored his first goal of 2010/11 from the penalty spot after a brace from Rankine, who was now obeying team orders. Following a 2-1 defeat at Fleetwood, though, Brodie was sold to Crawley for an undisclosed six-figure sum. Foyle accepted the club's decision despite losing his prize asset, saying, 'It was good money with the position the club is in. The McGill family are financing the whole club and, if they'd had another Clayton Donaldson and had got nothing, the chairman would have been criticised. It was a no-win situation. It has been accepted and we have got to move on.'

A club statement revealed that Brodie had turned down a new deal two months ago and added, 'The club had to let the player leave and accept a fee, bearing in mind that the player had asked to go.' Crawley boss Steve Evans went on to reveal that City chairman Jason McGill had contacted the Sussex club to make them aware of Brodie's availability. Brodie also insisted that he did not want to leave, saying, 'There had been two or three bids, which I turned down. I said I didn't want to leave the club. The club said the money was too good to turn down, which is fair enough. I said no three times before and, the fourth time, I had to think a lot about things. It has been probably on my mind for two weeks and it probably affected my performance on the pitch. I discussed it with family and friends and I broke the pros and cons down then I thought, "I am going to go." It is a fresh start and a new challenge.'

The whole saga dragged on further when Foyle suggested that supporter criticism might even have influenced Brodie's decision to move on, saying, 'He probably didn't want to leave but felt that he had to. He hasn't had a good start to the season, probably felt a bit down, and the challenge was there. After the stick he took on Monday down at Fleetwood – the crowd were telling him to get away – maybe that just tipped the scales. I can understand how footballers react, they react very quickly, but whether he has made the right decision only Richard will know.'

A difficult week for the club also saw Michael Gash plead guilty to affray and Rankine to a lesser charge in court following the city centre incident more than a year ago. They were later punished with community service and fines. All charges against Michael Ingham were dropped, however.

Former Leeds United and Port Vale striker Leon Constantine, brought in following Brodie's departure, went on to make a promising debut when, as a second-half substitute, he teed up a goal for Till and then got on the scoresheet himself in a 2-0 home win over Rushden & Diamonds. Constantine was on the scoresheet again, along with Rankine, as the Minstermen racked up a third straight home win and kept a fourth consecutive clean sheet after beating Hayes & Yeading United 2-0. The team were still without a win on their travels though following a 5-0 mauling at Mansfield. Former York winger Adam Smith opened the scoring and, then, after namesake Jonathan was sent off for the visitors for two bookable offences, the floodgates opened in the second half.

Foyle informed the local media by text message that he would not be commenting on the display afterwards and, three days later, the club announced that he had resigned from his position. The departing chief released a written statement but declined to make any further comment. It included the following:

Andy Porter and I have lived up here in York six nights a week and worked tirelessly to change the fortunes of the club to get it back to its position of challenging at the top of the league. We have certainly achieved this. With the money from the cup runs, Wembley visits and the sale of Richard Brodie, I know I leave the club in a much healthier position than when I arrived twenty months ago. Hopefully the club will move on and regain League status in the near future.

The reasons for Foyle's departure were never revealed and the board expressed their regret at his decision in a statement reading, 'We are very sad and disappointed Martin Foyle has left the club as manager. He has been a pleasure to work with and has made a highly positive contribution to York City over the past twenty months.' Assistant manager Porter, who was also unable to explain his long-time friend's resignation, took over for the next match and his audition for the full-time job could not have gone much better, with a 3-1 triumph at Gary Mills' Tamworth following goals from Rankine, Alex Lawless and debutant Jamal Fyfield – Foyle's last signing as City manager. Only adding to the mystery of his departure, meanwhile, Foyle contacted *The Press* to quell speculation suggesting he left Bootham Crescent to join another club. He said, 'Only one or two people know why I left the club and I haven't even told Andy Porter. I left for my own reasons, which I don't want to go into at this stage and I hope people can respect that.' A 0-0 draw with Darlington, followed by defeats at Eastbourne (2-1) and at home to Kettering (1-0), ended Porter's chances of filling the vacancy permanently.

Fleetwood forward Mark Beesley, brought in by Porter on loan, started against Kettering but proved no replacement for Brodie, nor did Constantine, despite his encouraging start to life at Bootham Crescent. Porter departed to be replaced by another caretaker chief Steve Torpey, who oversaw a third consecutive defeat – an awful 4-0 thumping at Newport that meant the club dropped to sixteenth in the table. 'I wanted the manager's job and it is hard then to go back to assistant,' Porter said, as he explained his decision to move on after learning he would not be considered for the position. 'It is a manager's job I am after. I have had a few years as assistant and I think I am ready.' Youth-team coach Torpey immediately made it clear that he was not interested in the vacancy, saying, 'I would like to manage at some stage but when I feel it's the right time. I don't feel I have the experience at this level at the moment.' After the Newport match, he added, 'I was looking forward to the game and felt the players were ready for action but obviously they were not.' It subsequently emerged that the City board had an approach rebuffed to talk to Darlington manager Mark Cooper about the job vacancy and, four days later, Tamworth boss and former European Cup winner Gary Mills was installed as the new first-team manager. Darron Gee also joined him from Tamworth as assistant manager. On the appointment, McGill said, 'Gary is a highly regarded manager who has extensive experience of Conference football and knows what is required to succeed in this league. We appointed Gary because of his considerable football knowledge and his enthusiasm and drive as a manager to replicate his successful playing career.'

An Internet poll conducted by *The Press*, at the time, revealed that 53 per cent of respondents believed Mills was the right man for the job, 12 per cent didn't and 35 per cent were not sure.

During a distinguished playing career, Mills became the youngest player to win a European Cup final at Nottingham Forest under the legendary Brian Clough and, during his first press conference, the new boss highlighted the importance of discipline and mutual respect at the club, saying, 'They obviously broke the mould when they made the genius Brian Clough and he was a one-off. I am my own man but, make no mistake, I learned a lot from him about discipline. The word discipline seems to frighten some people but it shouldn't. You should be proud of being disciplined. It makes you a better player and person. Players need to know what I expect from them and how to conduct themselves on and off the pitch. If they don't, then we have a problem.'

On respect for your fellow players and the importance of team spirit, Mills added, 'I played for a team at Forest that respected each other. We didn't necessarily like each other but we had lunch together and pulled up each other's socks and tucked each other's shirts in to win a game of football. I want that level of respect for one another at York City. You need to make players realise what they can achieve. I want every player to be the best they possibly can and they should all want that too. I want them to reach their maximum for this club and themselves.'

Outlining his ambitions for the club, Mills went on to add, 'Long term, we want to get out of this league. The club has been here too long but I'm sure everybody's heard all that before. There will be no promises from me about getting the club back into the Football League but that's our aim. The way to go about that is by working hard and being disciplined. We will also be trying to achieve what we want to achieve with a smile on our faces because I want a bunch of players who enjoy working for me.'

Unlike his predecessor Foyle, Mills also pointed out that he was not a diligent student of opposition teams, explaining, 'If the players are organised and regimental in what they do, you win matches, so I won't be worrying about the opposition.'

Mills' first match in charge ended the run of defeats but the team were held to a 1-1 home draw with Bath City. Delivering his verdict afterwards, the new manager said, 'There's a lot of work to be done. We got ourselves a point and I'm disappointed not to get three, but our second-half performance didn't warrant it. I would dread to think what the possession stats were in the second half. It was only my third day in the job but things have got to be sorted. We've got to start being organised and wanting the ball.'

A penalty from Rankine, playing alongside a striker in Gash, who had only two goals in forty-one games to his name, gave the hosts a first-half lead, but Alex Russell earned Bath a point just past the hour. Mills claimed his first win as City chief in the next match – a 2-0 triumph in the FA Cup fourth qualifying round at Kidderminster. His favoured 4-3-3 formation looked impressive as McDermott, brought back to the club after being released by Porter, pulled the strings in a surprise midfield anchorman role as the new manager showcased his pass-and-move football philosophy. Danny Racchi and Jonathan Smith were the marksmen, while new captain Chris Smith enjoyed a winning return on his second debut for the club. On installing the latter as his skipper in place of 'keeper Michael Ingham, Mills said, 'It might have raised a few eyebrows because he's just come into the club but I did it because I know what he's capable of and he organised the team superbly. I felt we needed somebody on the pitch to organise with a big mouth. I'm not a fan of goalkeeping captains because they're not close to the action on the field. I explained my decision to Michael and he understood and took it on the chin.'

Smith, who also played under Mills at Tamworth, extolled the 4-3-3 formation's virtues afterwards, saying, 'The manager has played the same system wherever he's been and it's a good one. It can be very hard to break down. There are different ways of playing 4-3-3 and it's all about getting his beliefs across.'

But Mills' frustration with City's misfiring front men was seen in the next match at Forest Green when Rankine and Constantine were substituted and, with Gash not even considered worthy of a place on the bench, midfielder Lawless played alongside winger Till in attack for the last twenty minutes. Lawless scored in the role but it proved little consolation during the 2-1 defeat. A smarting Rankine, however, responded with a performance full of power and potency to score two goals and set up the other for Chris Smith – all in the space of thirteen second-half minutes – as the Minstermen blew away League Two promotion hopefuls Rotherham during a 3-0 FA Cup first-round replay win after holding the Millers to a 0-0 draw in the initial tie. In between, Lawless left for Bedfordshire rivals Luton after handing in a transfer request and rejecting new contract talks with the Minstermen. A reluctant Mills sanctioned the transfer, adding, 'He has expressed on a few occasions that he wanted to go to Luton. It happened within a couple of days of me walking into the football club. I was still hoping that he would change his mind and sit down and discuss a new contract but he wanted to get away.' Long-serving defender David McGurk went on to put in another transfer request and also asked for permission to speak to Luton but Mills did not grant it, and turned down a £40,000 bid from the Hatters. Leicester winger Ashley Chambers, meanwhile, was brought in on loan, but a bid for Barrow striker Jason Walker proved unsuccessful and he went on to join Luton instead.

Along with their progress in the cup, City's fortunes in the league were also improving with a 4-0 thumping of hosts Rushden & Diamonds and a 2-0 home triumph over Southport lifting the team into the top half of the table. With Lawless gone, Trinidad and Tobago international midfielder Andre Boucaud arrived from Kettering and a 2-0 second-round FA Cup win at Darlington earned Mills his fourth consecutive victory and clean sheet thanks to goals from Djoumin Sangare – the latest player to fill the midfield anchorman role – and Chambers. The winning run came to an end but another shutout was achieved following a goalless stalemate on a freezing night in Kidderminster, and Mills picked up the Blue Square Bet Premier's November Manager of the Month award, while 'keeper Ingham earned the Player of the Month accolade after six clean sheets during a seven-game unbeaten run.

However, City were dumped out of the FA Trophy following a 1-0 first-round home defeat to Boston United and more Kenilworth Road controversy followed. Despite nationwide advance weather warnings from police for people to stay off the roads, Luton pressed ahead and attempted to stage their home match with City, even though the likes of nearby Premier League giants Arsenal and Chelsea called off their games – the latter with twenty-four hours' notice. Inevitably, the game was abandoned early in the second half following a heavy snowfall, with the scores deadlocked at 0-0. Most City fans then faced a torturous, ten-hour journey home, negotiating the gridlocked M1. Mills questioned the decision to start the game, saying, 'Everybody knew what the forecast was and how far our fans had to travel. We went down on Friday and our supporters will have set off at 7.30 a.m. in the morning. It's not just about getting people into matches, though, it's about making sure people get back home safely. You have to be sensible. We all knew the snow was going to come down and it's disappointing to go all the way to Luton and not be able to complete a game of football.'

City ensured they were quick out of the blocks in 2011, however, with a 3-0 victory at Gateshead's International Athletics Stadium. Hot-headed former Minsterman Craig Nelthorpe was sent off for the hosts after thirty minutes following reckless challenges on Chambers and Jonathan Smith. The team had now conceded just one goal in eight matches, including the abandoned Luton game with Chris Smith proving a steadying influence at the back.

Bolton subsequently required two late goals from England striker Kevin Davies and his £10-million striking partner Johan Elmander to beat City 2-0 in the third round of the FA Cup at the Reebok Stadium. Davies struck on eighty-three minutes and fellow substitute Elmander a minute from time but, earlier, Barrett had two glorious 6-yard chances to give the visitors the lead. He headed the first wide and was then denied by Hungarian 'keeper Adam Bogdan. City's 5,000 fans also saw Rankine unsettle England pair Gary Cahill and Zat Knight, while Jamie Reed made his debut for the visitors as a substitute just three days after playing his farewell game for Bangor City at Llanelli. Bolton boss Owen Coyle led the praise for the Minstermen afterwards, saying, 'I have to say York City deserve tremendous plaudits. I thought they were terrific, backed by a fantastic support that made for a good atmosphere. You almost sound like you're being patronising, but I thought they were brilliant and Gary Mills will be proud of how his players went about it. There were some nervous moments for us. We know we can perform better but I don't want to take anything away from York City.'

Davies also admitted that Bolton were 'relieved' to have made the fourth round, adding 'they gave us a tough time and will be going home disappointed'.

Mills rejected another bid from Luton for McGurk shortly afterwards and a 1-0 home win over Grimsby meant City had not conceded a league goal since October. That run ended at Histon but a 2-1 triumph lifted

Mills' men into the top ten. The manager's policy of not naming a goalkeeper on his substitutes' bench backfired in horrible fashion, however, during the rearranged match at Luton. Ingham was sent off after fourteen minutes and Chris Smith went on to concede four first-half goals after he donned the gloves with regrettable consequences until the break. Fellow centre-back Young took over for the second half and, given his disappointing defensive displays, arguably produced the best performance of his City career, only letting in one more goal, even though Jonathan Smith also received his marching orders on eighty-one minutes for a second bookable offence. McGurk received another red card after just seventy-one seconds for denying a goal-scoring opportunity at Southport led to a further heavy defeat as the Minstermen went down 4-0.

But the players bounced back in stunning style by inflicting a first league defeat since mid-November on title contenders AFC Wimbledon. Daniel Parslow, James Meredith, Rankine and Chambers were all on target during a fantastic 4-1 rout. Deadline-day signings Scott Kerr and Liam Darville also made their debuts in the match. On the capture of Lincoln City captain Kerr, Mills said, 'It's a big move for us to get him here. He knows we are ambitious and that I am building a squad that can get the club back into the League and he wants to help us do that. He's a leader and, as well as we have done since I have been here, I think we still need one or two more of them.'

The game represented a fitting tribute to the passing away of another club legend from the Happy Wanderers' era – all-time record goalscorer Norman Wilkinson. But Wimbledon gained revenge in the return fixture twelve days later, winning 1-0.

Ending all speculation of a move to Luton, McGurk then signed a new contract extension to keep him on the Minstermen's books until the summer of 2013. Explaining his decision, McGurk said, 'My reasons for changing my mind are pretty obvious. When I handed the request in, we were nineteenth in the league and I had better ambitions in terms of getting into the Football League. I didn't see us doing it and Luton are always up there so that's why I wanted to talk to them. The gaffer told me from day one, when I handed the request in, that we could get in the play-offs. I couldn't see it at the time because we were low on confidence and not playing well, but he has been proven right. We are nearly there and, even though there's a lot of hard work still to be done, the whole club has a belief we can get there.'

Mills, meanwhile, revealed that he wouldn't be recalling Gash from his loan period at Rushden & Diamonds after the £55,000 flop scored four times in a league match against Bath. 'I asked him to lose some weight to get in my team and he was given enough time to do that but nothing was forthcoming,' Mills said about Gash. 'When I came to the club in October, I could not afford to give players the equivalent of a pre-season to get fit.'

The club also revealed that they turned down an application from former England legend Paul Gascoigne for the managerial vacancy prior to appointing Mills. Commenting on Gazza's interest in the job, communications director Sophie Hicks said, 'We did not feel he was the right candidate for York City. We wanted somebody with experience of managing in the Conference and that's why we chose Gary Mills'.

City's home form remained majestic as a Reed brace secured an eighth successive league win at Bootham Crescent against Mansfield. The 2-1 triumph also closed the gap on Kidderminster, in the last play-off place, to four points. Afterwards, Mills even signalled his intention to finish in the division's top three. A 1-0 victory over Histon made it nine home wins on the trot as Reed, despite only starting five matches since his move from Bangor, grabbed his sixth goal of the season. But Rankine's eighty-eighth minute penalty miss in a 1-1 draw at Kettering, with Reed on target again, cost City two vital points as the team's play-off push entered its final month. The winning home sequence also came to an end when champions-elect Crawley grabbed a fortunate deflected second-half equaliser from Sergio Torres to extend their unbeaten league run to a twenty-fourth game. Jonathan Smith had earlier given the hosts a fourteenth-minute lead.

City's season-long struggle to convert chances ultimately cost the team during a damaging 2-1 home defeat to Tamworth, with the club boasting the fifth-lowest goals for column in the division after that match. City old boy Courtney, playing at centre-back, surprisingly shackled Rankine, as he chose the fixture to deliver his best-ever Bootham Crescent performance. Fellow former Minstermen Ben Wilkinson and Christian Smith also impressed for the visitors. Prior to the match, it had emerged that Aldershot were interested in signing out-of-contract striker Rankine but it was Wilkinson, who hadn't netted in eleven home outings for the Minstermen, who opened the scoring after twenty-six minutes. Kyle Perry added a second after the break as the hosts conceded two goals at home for the first time since the opening day of the season, meaning Constantine's last-minute header was a mere consolation.

Another eventful match against Luton saw hosts City win 1-0 thanks to Reed's ninth goal of the season, despite being reduced to ten men after Kerr's dismissal for two bookable offences midway through the second period. Hatters manager Gary Brabin was also sent from the dugout after attempting to pick a fight with City assistant manager Darron Gee. A scuffle with stewards, which led to Brabin's arrest, ensued down in the players' tunnel, with Luton captain George Pilkington also cautioned for leaving the pitch as he attempted to pacify the situation. Brabin was later cleared of assault but found guilty of threatening behaviour and fined.

A patched-up City, fielding left-backs Fyfield and Meredith in the centre of defence and missing the suspended Kerr, then went down 2-1 at Darlington in their next fixture to leave the team requiring an Easter miracle to reach the play-offs with two games to play. That remote hope was ended as the Minstermen failed to score at home for the first time under Mills in a goalless draw with Cambridge.

The result meant, however, that the team had equalled a club record of just thirteen home goals conceded in a league season, taking their place in the history books alongside the 1993/94 team that boasted the likes of club favourites Dean Kiely, Andy McMillan, Steve Tutill, Wayne Hall and Paul Stancliffe. Mills praised the club's fans as an eighth season of Conference football was confirmed and immediately set his sights on winning the title next time out:

This is a fantastic club and the supporters are superb. It's another season that we haven't got out of this league and that's hard for them to take but they keep coming and paying their money week in, week out so I want to say a big thank you to all of them. They've made myself and Darron welcome from day one and we've worked so hard to get this club where we all want it to be. I'm just glad we kept the season alive for them for so long. In the short space of time I have been here I have given this club expectation. They are expecting better next season and I want to win the title.

When I was at Tamworth, probably a bit more tongue in cheek, I wanted to win the title. Now I am at a football club where we can win the title if I get the squad right – because we are a big enough club. I know what the budget is and the budget is okay. It is about how I spend it. It's down to me and my assistant and everyone around the football club that I get in the right players and I rebuild a side for next season.

City closed the season by becoming only the second team, after Grimsby, to avoid defeat in either of their games against runaway champions Crawley. As at Bootham Crescent, City took the lead against the Sussex side, courtesy of a David Hunt own goal. But Levi Mackin's reckless lunge handed Tubbs the second-half opportunity to rescue a point for the hosts with his fortieth goal of the season from the penalty spot. It denied the visitors a chance to claim their twenty-third clean sheet of the campaign.

The Minstermen, who ended the season eighth, had now witnessed Crawley, Oxford and Stevenage all celebrate promotion in their final fixtures of the last three seasons. The team also finished the campaign having beaten five of the seven teams that finished above them and remained undefeated against the other two. 'Since October, we have proven we can win football matches,' concluded a positive Mills.

Above: Gary Mills on his first day of work at Bootham Crescent. (Michael Tipping)

Left: Michael Rankine competes for possession with England defender Gary Cahill in the FA Cup third round at Bolton. (Nigel Holland)

Above: Neil Barrett misses a great chance to open the scoring at the Reebok Stadium. (Nigel Holland)

Right: And then covers his mouth in shock. (Nigel Holland)

8

'A TERRIFIC TREBLE'

Sentimentality played no part in Gary Mills' plans for the 2011/12 season.

Neil Barrett, Chris Carruthers, Levi Mackin, Michael Rankine and Michael Gash – all members of the 2010 play-off final side – failed to make the retained list. Mills did admit, however, that he had made his first 'major signing' of the summer when James Meredith, another player from that team, agreed a new one-year deal with the club, despite interest in his services from Chesterfield, Crewe and Kilmarnock. Leon Constantine and Peter Till were amongst other notable departures and Rankine, who turned down a contract extension at the turn of the year, went on to sign for Aldershot. Ashley Chambers, though, turned his loan stay from Leicester into a permanent move and striker Liam Henderson arrived on a two-year deal from Watford, despite an uninspiring record of no goals in fifty senior outings.

Winger Matty Blair was the next recruit from Kidderminster. On his strengths, the former Racing Club Warwick amateur said, 'I bring pace, work-rate, fitness and, I'd like to say, goals.' Mills' long pursuit of Jason Walker also came to a happy conclusion when he arrived from Luton in a £60,000 deal. The delighted City boss said, 'It's no secret that one of the first conversations I had with the chairman when I came here was "Can we go and sign Jason Walker?" I rate him very highly. He will give us goals, which is something we needed to address after last season. He also has a great work ethic and desire for the game.

'We have had to pay a good fee for him, which shows the ambition of the club and the chairman. Good strikers don't come cheaply and we have had to up our offers to eventually get him here. Luton have signed another striker in Rushden's Aaron O'Connor but, if I was them, I wouldn't have wanted to lose Jason.'

Despite Luton being installed as title favourites and City placed fifth in the betting market, Walker insisted, 'Luton are a big club but so are York. The club has a long Football League history too and this is nowhere near a backward step for me.'

Teenage Blackburn Rovers midfielder Michael Potts was the next new addition, followed by twenty-one-year-old Glenn Hoddle Academy graduate Adriano Moke and former Histon right-back Lanre Oyebanjo. Midfielder Jonathan Smith left for Swindon, though, in a £30,000 deal, while veteran Paul Musselwhite was brought in for a dual role as goalkeeping coach and playing cover for Michael Ingham. Newcastle United reserve Paddy McLaughlin became Mills' final summer signing.

Walker made a dream City debut when his late brace secured a 2-1 win at ten-man Ebbsfleet. The new striker displayed great nerve to level the scores from the spot, having seen his last penalty saved in former club Luton's play-off final shoot-out defeat to AFC Wimbledon. He then headed in a brilliant winning goal from an excellent cross by fellow debutant Oyebanjo. The victory represented only the second time in eight years as a Conference club that City had tasted victory on the opening day of the season.

Another win at Barrow followed before Craig Farrell returned to Bootham Crescent to clinch a surprise 1-0 victory for new team Telford. Farrell, who only managed one goal at Bootham Cresecent during his last twelve months at the club, scored with his first touch after entering the action as an eighty-fourth-minute substitute. City bounced back by storming to a 5-1 win at crisis club Kettering thanks to Andre Boucaud, Walker (2), Moke and new signing Danny Pilkington.

The Minstermen slumped to back-to-back home defeats for the first time under Mills, however, when Alfreton took the points in a 1-0 win as another Bootham Crescent old boy Mackin scored from the spot. Mackin, who only managed two goals in two and a half years for City, ensured that no home game had passed in 2011/12 by that stage without an ex-player getting on the scoresheet, following on from Farrell and Adam Boyes for Barrow. A nightmare return to Tamworth for Chris Smith then saw the City skipper concede two penalties that were both converted in a 2-1 win for the home side.

The team dropped to fourteenth in the table and, with doubters and doomsayers starting to question Mills' side, the City chief responded, 'I don't like to lose any game so to lose back-to-back matches in the manner that we have hurts me as manager. We've lost two games that were important to us and not played as well as we wanted to, but it's not a major crisis.' Consequently, an unconvincing home win over bottom-of-the-table Bath, courtesy of Jamie Reed's eighty-eighth-minute strike, then proved a pivotal moment in City's season. Visiting winger Ben Swallow had earlier seen a penalty saved by Ingham. City went on to shock league leaders Wrexham by cantering to a 3-0 win at the Racecourse Ground with McLaughlin, Chambers and Reed all netting within the first twenty-four minutes. McLaughlin, Boucaud and Scott Kerr were imperious in the middle of the park for the visitors and kept possession in a fashion that bordered on exhibition football at times. Another devastating 3-0 victory - this time completed by half-time – saw City sweep aside a second promotion rival in Luton at Bootham Crescent with Chambers (two) and Walker on target.

But the curse of the former player struck again at the end of September when one-time, on-loan Minsterman Jon Shaw scored a hat-trick as Gateshead clinched a 3-2 home win over Mills' team.

Off the pitch, meanwhile, Oakgate's planning application for a new community sports stadium and shopping park at Monks Cross was submitted, with chairman Jason McGill outlining the repercussions if it was rejected. He warned, 'This is our last chance and only realistic opportunity of getting a community stadium for York. Without this stadium, the club could be homeless and we would certainly have to go part-time the season after next, which would be disastrous for the club and the ambitions of our supporters.'

Everything remained positive on the field, however, with Walker becoming the first City player to hit ten goals by 1 October after netting in a 2-1 win at Stockport. He beat the previous record, held by Arthur Bottom and Jimmy Weir, by a day. An indication of Mills' rising reputation was provided when he was linked by one national newspaper to the vacancy at his former club Nottingham Forest following the end of Steve McClaren's brief spell at the City Ground helm. He immediately distanced himself from the speculation, however, saying, 'When your name gets linked with other clubs, it means you're doing something right so that's pleasing. I'm a human being and it's always flattering when it happens but I don't want anybody here to think I'm looking beyond York City, because I'm not. I have a personal drive to get this club back in the Football League and that's all I'm concentrating on. Next week, I'll have been here a year and it's been a fantastic twelve months. I honestly feel we have progressed during that time and we have to keep progressing.'

That progress was palpable when Braintree were seen off 6-2 at Bootham Crescent in the next game. It was the first time the club had scored six goals in a league game since 1985. Chambers (two), McLaughlin, Fyfield, Walker and Moke were the marksmen with Braintree also helping contribute to the highest aggregate scoreline at Bootham Crescent since 1956 when Southport were trounced 9-1.

Walker went on to score a sensational overhead kick in a pulsating 2-1 home victory over Grimsby. It became one of the most-watched strikes of its kind since Pele's Escape to Victory effort, attracting 165,000 hits on Youtube within a week. As a result, Chambers' winning goal on eighty-six minutes was somewhat overshadowed. Gash, though, became the fourth City old boy to score at Bootham Crescent during the season, as his Cambridge United team converted their only two chances of the night to steal a 2-2 draw against the Minstermen. City created twenty-two opportunities, but had to wait for Walker's second goal of the game to earn a point in the eighty-ninth minute. Following an impressive 4-2 win at Hayes & Yeading United, Mills then decided to make seven changes to the side that had started the previous six games for an FA Cup fourth qualifying round trip to table-topping Wrexham. An eighty-first-minute David McGurk own goal handed the hosts a 2-1 win after McLaughlin had earlier levelled the scores.

Three consecutive draws followed, with the second against Barrow seeing Walker and Boucaud both sent off – the first for a late challenge and the second for his involvement in the ensuing melee. Both picked up three-game bans. Sophie Hicks, meanwhile, hit out at city-centre retailers objecting to the Monks Cross community stadium enabling developments, saying, 'Personally, I believe it is ridiculous to state York city centre will be destroyed by the existence of a Marks & Spencer store and a John Lewis store at Monks Cross. It is utter nonsense. What about the 1,000 jobs and £87-million investment this development will bring to York in this time of austerity when additional employment is essential and should not be turned away?'

Former council leader Steve Galloway had earlier said the objectors were promoting 'distorted arguments fuelled by vested interests'.

Even without their leading marksman Walker and midfield magician Boucaud, City then crushed Kettering 7-0 with the appearance of six different players on the scoresheet – Reed (two), Jon Challinor, Blair, McLaughlin, Chambers and Moses Ashikodi – representing a club record. The victory was also the club's second-biggest ever. Ahead of a first-round home tie with Solihull Moors, meanwhile, Mills signalled his intention to win the FA Trophy, saying, 'I want to get this club to Wembley again but win there this time and every player at the club should be committed to wanting to do that. I'm not just saying that because it's the right thing to say, I'm saying it because it's a fantastic competition that gives everybody the chance to end the season at our national stadium.'

It required a scrambled Challinor equaliser in the third minute of stoppage time, however, to clinch a 2-2 draw at Bootham Crescent. Goals from Blair (two) and Smith then secured a more straightforward 3-0 win in the replay. Kidderminster, however, inflicted a first league defeat on City in thirteen games when they won 3-2 at Bootham Crescent. It ended the club's longest run without a league loss in twenty-five years. Henderson, briefly recalled from a loan spell at Forest Green, went on to score an equaliser at Mansfield to ensure the Minstermen ended 2011 with a fourth consecutive away draw.

Another draw with the Stags – this time 2-2 after Jamal Fyfield's injury-time equaliser – then saw City kick off 2012 having failed to win for three successive home games for the first time under Mills. With the transfer window having reopened, Mills insisted that he would not part with star striker Walker, who had been heavily scouted by Sheffield Wednesday, for £2 million. 'We're not interested in any offer for him even if it was a couple of million,' the manager said. 'He is not going and that's coming from both the chairman and me. We're both adamant that's the case.'

City went on to score six goals away from home for the first time since an FA Cup tie at South Shields in 1968 when they beat Salisbury 6-2 in the second round of the Trophy. Blair and McLaughlin both scored twice and were joined on the scoresheet by Reed and new signing Matthew Blinkhorn. A phenomenal performance by Blair, during a 3-2 home win over Ebbsfleet, then led Mills to label the former Kidderminster winger 'Forrest Gump' due to his non-stop running. Blair bagged a brace for the third consecutive match, taking his tally to twelve from the last ten games, which compensated for the loss of an injured Walker. The victory was achieved despite transfer-window signing Scott Brown being sent off for a reckless challenge after only fifteen minutes, with Blair doing the running of two men to negate the numerical disadvantage. Left-back Meredith also netted a rare goal, set up by the irrepressible Blair. On Blair's new nickname, Mills laughed: 'He's like Forrest Gump – he didn't stop running all game and was unbelievable. I was shouting "run Forrest, run" from the dugout and, even when you didn't think he'd get to the ball first sometimes, he did. It was amazing really. When you have somebody with his heart, you're always going to be more than capable of getting something out of any game.'

As the January transfer window closed, Boucaud left in a £25,000 move to Luton, having fallen out of favour under Mills despite his inspirational early-season form. Explaining the transfer, Mills said, 'I have to make big decisions and to pick the right players for this football club. Luton expressed an interest in Andre and I felt it was the right time for him to move on as it allows me to potentially strengthen the team in other areas.' Sheffield United utility man Erik Tonne subsequently arrived on loan and Bristol Rovers winger Ben Swallow was also recruited, along with free agent Chris Doig – a former Nottingham Forest centre-back – and Middlesbrough defender Ben Gibson, who joined on loan with City beating Hibernian to his signature. Asked in mid-February for the first time about the prospect of his team pulling off a Wembley double, Mills said, 'If we went and did that, then blimey, it would be absolutely fantastic.'

That possibility took another step towards reality when Blair was on target again as the Minstermen edged past Ebbsfleet 1-0 in the third round of the FA Trophy at Bootham Crescent. Walker, though, missed a late penalty on his return to the starting line-up after an eight-game absence due to groin problems. The clean sheet was Ingham's eighty-second for the club, moving him level with Dean Kiely in the all-time list and only trailing Happy Wanderers legend Tommy Forgan, whose club record stands at 120. The longest unbeaten run in Mills' City managerial career ended with a 2-1 home defeat to Gateshead, who completed the double over their North Yorkshire rivals. It was the Minstermen's first loss in ten games, with Micky Cummins' brace securing the points despite Reed's reply. Kerr, meanwhile, ended a 121-game run without a goal with an eighty-third-minute header that clinched a 1-0 FA Trophy quarter-final victory at Grimsby. City became the first team to beat Grimsby, other than Salisbury who required extra time, in twenty-three matches.

Mills also employed full-back Meredith in a midfield role for the first time with encouraging results. Kerr speculated afterwards that fate might be playing its part in City's Trophy triumphs, saying, 'When you go all the way in cup competitions, I think all teams look back at little things along the way that make you wonder whether your name was written on the trophy. We were out of the competition in the first round before Jon Challinor scored with the last kick of the game and, when I then get the winning goal in the quarter-final, you do think that might be the case but there's still plenty of work to do before that can happen.'

Commenting on the possibility of reaching the final, Kerr added, 'I've had a good career but I've never played at Wembley so it would be a massive deal for me to do that.' Walker then scored for the first time in ten matches – a run stretching back to October – when he converted a penalty during a 2-0 home win over Hayes & Yeading United. Mills, though, failed in a third attempt to beat his former club Tamworth, but at least won a point from a 0-0 home draw, following two poor defeats previously.

In the Trophy semi-finals, City were pitted against bitter rivals Luton, but only managed a 1-0 first-leg victory at Bootham Crescent over a visiting team reduced to nine men for forty minutes, in a typically tempestuous affair between the two clubs. Reed scored from the penalty spot on fourteen minutes after Jake Howells was sent off for deliberate handball. Midfielder Keith Keane also headed for an early shower on fifty-five minutes following two bookable offences. Afterwards, Mills railed against home fans, who barracked City players at the final whistle. In an out-of-character tirade, the City boss fumed, 'If we put nine men behind the ball then I'd like to see how many times the opposition score. I'd be disappointed if we let in two or three and, fair play to them, they defended well. Yes, we could have done better in situations but to get booed off is beyond me. We are taking a lead into the second leg of the FA Trophy semi-final and to get booed for that is unbelievable.'

Prior to the return leg, the Minstermen went on to produce their most thrilling performance of the season in a 3-2 midweek victory at Grimsby, which was settled by Fyfield's brilliant ninety-third-minute solo goal. Reed and Smith's earlier goals had been cancelled out by Anthony Elding and Michael Coulson replies, but Fyfield sprinted 60 yards with the ball before firing in from the edge of the Mariners' box. In the second leg of the Trophy semi-final, Blair's ninetieth-minute header from Fyfield's fantastic left-wing cross secured a 2-1 aggregate victory over a crestfallen Luton at Kenilworth Road. It was the first goal Luton had conceded at home in ten games and Robbie Willmott had earlier levelled the tie on forty-three minutes.

City suffered a blow, however, when it was revealed that Kerr would miss the rest of the season, with the talismanic midfielder suffering knee ligament damage following a first-half clash with Keane. At the final whistle, chairman Jason McGill emphasised the financial importance of Blair's goal, saying, 'It will be worth around £200,000 to us, which is very significant at our level. It's no secret the club loses around £300,000 at Bootham Crescent every season to keep running a full-time professional side, a youth team and a community department. At the start of every campaign, we know those will be the losses in the Blue Square Bet Premier if we do not get to the Trophy final, the third round of the FA Cup or, of course, promoted. So, when you get days like this, the board of directors feel vindicated in a way for continuing to aspire to where we want to be.'

Reflecting afterwards, a modest Blair added, 'I started off as a nobody really and I've worked my way up. If you had told me four years ago that I'd be playing at Wembley when I was playing for Racing Club Warwick with a man and his dog watching I'd have punched you.' His son's goal provided a bittersweet moment, however, for Blair's father Andy – a member of Aston Villa's 1981/82 European Cup-winning squad. 'When I scored the goal, he was the first down to the front and got pushed,' Blair junior recounted. 'He went over, broke his metatarsal and will be in plaster for six months but I think he would take that again if he had to.' A delighted Mills added, 'It means everything and feels great to get to the final of such a prestigious competition at Wembley – it really does.' The Minstermen went on to clinch a 2-1 league win at Kenilworth Road, with late goals from McLaughlin and Meredith sinking the Bedfordshire play-off rivals after Andre Gray had given the Hatters a fifth-minute lead. Frustrated home fans directed 'You're Getting Sacked In the Morning' chants at beleaguered boss Brabin and got their wish soon afterwards.

City's record undefeated run of away results ended, though, after a 2-1 defeat in Newport. Mills' players had not lost any of their previous thirteen fixtures on the road. Either side of a belting McLaughlin free-kick, goals by Nat Jarvis and substitute Romone Rose earned the relegation-threatened Exiles maximum points. Richard Brodie then returned to Bootham Crescent to fire his new club Fleetwood to within one win of the Blue Square Bet Premier title. Entering the action as a second-half substitute, Brodie cut inside Doig and fired past former teammate Ingham from 10 yards with his left foot.

City moved on, undeterred, to Alfreton, where Daniel Parslow starred in the midfield-holding role, which had proven difficult to fill since Kerr's injury and the visitors enjoyed a 2-0 win. Walker then scored the club's twenty-third second half goal in seventeen matches – compared to just three before the interval during that time – to secure a 1-1 home draw with Newport.

With three fixtures of the regular season remaining and the club's play-off fate yet to be decided, an untimely ankle injury to ever-present Ingham, though, meant goalkeeper coach Musselwhite was then thrown in for his first professional start for almost six years. At forty-three, Musselwhite became the oldest player to turn out for the club, beating a sixty-two-year-old record set by fellow 'keeper Matt Middleton, who was a mere forty-two when he played his last game for City. The club suffered a fortieth-minute blow on Musselwhite's debut at Cambridge when Gibson was sent off for a reckless challenge on Lee Thorpe. But the visitors held their nerve and clinched a crucial victory courtesy of Walker's eighteenth goal of the season – a terrific strike on the counter attack.

Walker's blushes were spared in the next game, however, when he somehow contrived to hit the bar from 3 yards in front of an empty net at Braintree. It was left to utility man Tonne, who had played a minor role since his loan arrival from Sheffield United, to become the unlikely hero when he broke the deadlock on seventy-five minutes to secure a play-off place moments after being hailed from the bench. Earlier, Braintree had seen striker Sean Marks sent off in controversial circumstances during the first half. Marks went down in the box after colliding with Musselwhite, leading to anxious moments as home players and supporters screamed for a penalty. The possible ramifications of a penalty in the game, as well as a red card and subsequent suspension for Musselwhite with Ingham still injured, were unthinkable, but referee Stephen Martin chose instead to caution Marks for a second time for alleged simulation and it was the Braintree forward who trudged off for an early bath.

The win set another new club record too, with City having only lost three away games during their league campaign, beating the previous lowest tally set by Tom Johnson's 1973/74 side. Tonne's goal also provided another fitting tribute to an FA Cup semi-final hero. Arthur Bottom – the club's greatest-ever signing from Bramall Lane – had passed away in the build up to the match. A delighted Mills said afterwards, 'We're in the FA Trophy final and in the play-offs with a chance of getting to Wembley twice. It's been a fantastic season and we want to finish it off in the right way now.' On Musselwhite's unexpected contribution to the end-of-season promotion push, Mills added, 'Hopefully, things will improve this week and Michael Ingham will be okay but, if not, the coolest man at the club will continue in goal. Everybody thought Inghy's injury might have put a downer on our chances of getting the points we needed to reach the play-offs. Luton and Kidderminster probably looked at it and said "they've lost their 'keeper and have only got somebody who's going on forty-four and looks like he enjoys his Burger Kings and McDonalds a bit too much", but he's been absolutely fantastic. He's a great bloke to have on my coaching staff and he's not let us down during the last two games. It wouldn't faze me playing him at Wembley if we needed to. We would see how cool he was then. But I know that, if he has to go in, he will do well.'

Musselwhite went on to become the proud owner of a second club record. This one had nothing to do with his 1960s birth certificate, as a 1-0 home victory over Forest Green, secured by an eighty-second-minute Moke strike, meant he became the first-ever 'keeper to enjoy three clean sheets during his opening three matches for the Minstermen. The three consecutive 1-0 triumphs also meant Mills' men finished the season with their first consecutive hat-trick of league wins in the campaign.

Prior to the start of the play-offs, captain Chris Smith spoke of his desire for redemption after being a member of the York squad that was relegated from the Football League back in 2004 during his first spell with the club. In between times, Smith had plied his trade at non-League level and even on a part-time basis, combining playing duties with work as a plasterer, before his return to North Yorkshire.' It was a horrible, horrible feeling to get relegated,' Smith recalled. 'At any level, it's a bad experience but, to come out of the League, is such a hard thing to deal with and not a good thing to have on your CV. I never thought then that I would be coming back years later as captain with the chance of taking the team back up at Wembley. I would have loved to feel that might happen, but never thought it would be the case. It's such a nice feeling now that I might be able to repay the club for being a member of that squad. If we can win two finals at Wembley, I'm sure that will all be forgotten about.'

In the play-off semi-finals, City were paired with a Mansfield team that had won thirteen of their last fifteen fixtures, but the honours were even during a 1-1 draw in the first leg at Bootham Crescent. Mansfield suffered a blow, however, when thirty-goal top-scorer Matt Green was sent off for two bookable offences and, therefore, picked up a ban for the return leg. Ross Dyer had earlier headed the Stags in front midway through the first half, beating a fit-again Ingham, but Exodus Geohaghon's own goal, following a Challinor cross, levelled the scores before the break. At the end of the game, Mills remained confident of second-leg success, saying, 'If we are patient and compete with them, I think we will go through.' They proved prophetic words, as City required extra-time before another header by Blair secured a second Wembley final place. Blair met a 111th-minute left-wing cross at the far post in a near carbon copy of his decisive semi-final Trophy goal at Kenwilworth Road. On this occasion, though, Walker delivered the cross, not Fyfield.

The victory meant the Minstermen had won at the four most hostile venues in the Conference – Mansfield, Luton, Wrexham and Grimsby – during the course of the campaign. It was also the first time Mansfield had been beaten at home in six months and thirteen games. A jubilant Mills said, 'We are going to Wembley twice in a week. That doesn't happen to many football clubs and how good does it feel?' An emotional Jason McGill, whose nerves were shredded by the tense encounter, added, 'It was an awful occasion. I don't really enjoy the games as I am watching them, certainly at the business end of the season. There was nothing between the two teams in all the games we played and I think that showed. That moment of brilliance won the game, a wonderful header from Matty Blair to get the win.'

The team left Field Mill for the Field of Dreams, where Newport lay in wait first for the final of the FA Trophy. Wembley was hosting its 100th match since being redeveloped, but the game's first hour struggled to live up to the occasion. Typically, however, City scored twice after the break, meaning twenty-eight of their last thirty-three goals had come in the second half of matches. First, Chambers released Blair with a perfectly weighted pass that lured County 'keeper Glyn Thompson off his line and out of his penalty box. The winger then lifted the ball over Thompson to open the scoring with his team's 100th goal of 2011/12. Chambers also created the second as he swapped passes with McLaughlin before racing down the right flank and delivering a low cross that gave Oyebanjo, converted from right back into midfield, a tap in. Newport defender Ismail Yakubu headed against the post late on, but City finished deserved winners.

Putting a smile back on people's faces had been Mills' mission statement on taking over at Bootham Crescent. Well, if the famous Wembley arch had been tipped upside down, that was about the size of the average City fan's grin after their team ended a ninety year wait to win their first national knockout competition. The 2-0 triumph also exorcised the memories of the club's last two trips to the hallowed home of English football. Communications director Sophie Hicks said afterwards, 'I hope we have made the people of York proud by bringing silverware home. You have got to think back to the dark days of ten years ago, when we potentially didn't have a football club. Everybody has worked so hard to bring York City back from that point and now we are reaping the rewards.'

Skipper Smith took injured vice-captain Kerr up with him as he lifted the Trophy and said, 'He's been the player of the year and brilliant all season. You wish none of your teammates to be in that situation. Let's not beat about the bush, he would have been playing had he been fit. He said he wasn't fussed and "I'll stay at the back" but I thought "you deserve it". It has been a horrible thing for him to go through. He has dealt with it brilliantly. I wanted him to be there to lift that cup.'

Keeper Ingham also reflected on the difference between the club's latest trip to Wembley and their two previous visits. 'It felt like sprinting up those steps this time,' he said of the famous climb up to the Royal Box. 'Before it felt like climbing up a mountain. It is well documented about my mistake last time here (against Oxford) and I got a bit of stick for it, but I have put a lot of demons to bed. I've kept a clean sheet at Wembley in my career now and I have won my first trophy in my career and you can't beat it.'

Double-assist-provider Chambers added, 'I know I should score more but to set up a goal is great and to be involved in the two goals at Wembley is great.'

On winning his first silverware as a professional and the prospect of becoming a league player for the first time, the experienced Challinor – a non-contract player with crisis club Kettering during the first two months of the season – added, 'To win something for the first time at thirty-one means everything to me but to win promotion would be another thing all together. It would cap a great season because I have come back from nowhere to get this opportunity. I thought I was on the scrapheap to be honest.'

Mills spoke afterwards of a successful start to a momentous nine days for the club, saying, 'I just hope this is the beginning of many things for this football club. It's a fantastic club and a great city full of lovely people. The ultimate aim is to get promoted but we talked about winning the Trophy from the moment we entered the competition and we were thirty seconds away from getting knocked out in the first game so to win it feels great and a superb start to a massive nine days for us. On Thursday, we will learn whether the stadium has been given the go-ahead and it is clear we have to move on.

'It's not just about people coming through the turnstiles in football any more. You need more to progress and even survive as we have seen with a lot of teams so it's a big day on Thursday and a massive one on Sunday. My job at the start of the season was to get York City promoted and we want to pull that off.'

On the possible advantage the victory against Newport could provide over play-off final opponents Luton, Mills added, 'The players now know what it feels like to win at Wembley and that's a great thing to take into the next match.'

He also believed past results between the two teams could have a bearing as well, saying, 'Every game we have played against Luton we have had to be at our best because we know they are a strong side. We have proved that our best has been good enough. Why not do our best again and go and beat them again on Sunday? They have got a point to prove because they haven't beaten us. They have got that added pressure of trying to do that. I think they will probably be hurt that when they have played York City we have done very well against them. I've got to make sure that doesn't change on Sunday.'

Underlining what victory would mean to Mills, still the youngest-ever player to win a European Cup or Champions League final, the manager added, 'It will certainly be the proudest moment of my footballing career – including my playing career – to get this football club into the Football League – without doubt.'

After planning permission is obtained for the community stadium at Monks Cross, the stage is then set for the club to complete an historic, nine-day hat-trick. Mills did not need to worry about former midfielder Boucaud tormenting his old teammates in the final with the Trinidad and Tobago international firmly out of favour at Kenilworth Road, having failed to make the previous six Hatters squads. Prior to his York departure, Boucaud had been an integral member of a midfield triumvirate, alongside Kerr and McLaughlin, that had passed a succession of teams into submission during those early summer and autumn days. But, while the second half of the campaign had been less aesthetically pleasing, Mills regularly demonstrated the flexibility of his squad and, for the final, caused a surprise by dropping McLaughlin and filling his midfield engine room with two full-backs, Meredith and Oyebanjo, and a centre-half Parslow.

Mills' team had proven through the season that they could compensate for a loss of craft with bundles of graft, as well as a self-belief that had seen the team recover a sensational seventeen points from losing positions with seven of those collected courtesy of injury-time goals. That character had shone through too in the play-off semi-final with City prevailing after trailing against Mansfield, not to mention in the FA Trophy when Challinor's last-gasp equaliser prevented the team from falling at the first hurdle.

There was, therefore, no cause for panic among the Minstermen faithful when, buoyed by a raucous 30,000 supporters, Luton took the lead after just seventy-one seconds when Gray steered a composed 10-yard finish in off Ingham's left-hand post. City, cheered on by their 9,000 followers, remained unflustered and Walker made a nonsense of the seven-inch difference between himself and former on-loan Minsterman Janos Kovacs by outjumping the hulking Hungarian defender and winning a header that back-peddaling Hatters 'keeper Mark Tyler did well to tip over. The equaliser arrived on twenty-six minutes when Keane hacked down Challinor as he burst down the right wing to collect a Blair through ball. Oyebanjo curled the subsequent free-kick to the far post, where Smith cushioned the ball down on his chest before aiming it back towards the penalty spot. There, steaming in, came Chambers who, after the ball bounced invitingly up off the hallowed turf, smashed a rising 12-yard drive into the roof of a helpless Tyler's net to claim his tenth goal of the campaign.

A minute into the second half, Blair then pounced to add yet another vital goal to his burgeoning collection. Having netted the decisive headers to send his team to Wembley twice and broken the deadlock in the FA Trophy final, Blair's latest stratospheric strike proved his most important. The former Racing Club Warwick winger side-footed through Tyler's legs from 4 yards after Parslow had helped on Oyebanjo's right-wing long throw with his head at the near post. Television replays later confirmed Blair was clearly 2 yards offside, but the flag stayed down and the Minstermen had a lead to defend, which they did with typical grit.

An aggrieved Luton still had forty minutes to muster up an equaliser but couldn't. Oyebanjo made two brave and unlikely interceptions to deny Craig McAllister and John-Paul Kissock, while Gray took swipes at the ball with both his left and right feet 3 yards in front of Ingham's goal but completely missed it on both occasions. After making his second successful climb to the Royal Box on consecutive weekends, a jubilant Smith said, 'It's unbelievable to be back in the League. It feels like I have repaid some of the fans. I am not saying it was all my fault but I was part of that squad that got relegated. Now, I feel the club is in a more stable position. It has got the go-ahead for the stadium and it is certainly a better team – no disrespect to the other one I was in.'

Oyebanjo added, 'I've played four seasons in the Conference and to finally say you're a League player – it's truly beautiful. Those drinks by the pool over the summer will taste so much better.'

Blair, reflecting on his unbelievable run of crucial goals, said, 'Luton away in the semi-final of the Trophy had been the best goal I ever scored, the most valuable and the most precious to me. It got better at Mansfield, it got better in the Trophy and it has got better again.' Jason McGill, fighting back the tears again, said, 'This provides us with financial security going forward. I don't see why we can't operate, break even, invest in the squad and put together a team that can compete in League Two. I truly believe with the structure we have got that we are a top half of League One team.'

Beaten Luton boss Paul Buckle was unhappy with Blair's winning goal but was generous in defeat, saying, 'We needed a bit of luck but York got it and I don't begrudge them the win because they played very well and deserved that second goal on the balance of play.' A jubilant Mills, meanwhile, declared, 'To come to Wembley two weekends running and do the double is an incredible feeling. In fact, with the ground announcement, it's been a terrific treble and probably the best hat-trick ever at York City Football Club.'

At the final whistle, an emotional Mills had sunk to his knees and looked to the sky, while City's players and supporters kicked off delirious celebrations.

Who could blame them? It had been a long time coming.

Few needed reminding that the Minstermen's last Football League opponents, Swansea, had climbed to football's top table in the intervening period. City might never grace the same heights as the top-flight Welsh side but, as a Conference swansong, their last nine days as a non-League football club had felt every bit as historic. 'It's Getting Better', by York's own Shed Seven, had been belted out before the game but, in truth, football does not get much better. The club had been promoted for the first time in nineteen years and Bradford not Braintree now awaited in their 2012/13 fixture list.

Speaking on the open-top bus as thousands of people turned up to celebrate the team's achievements, Mills said, 'I've been here eighteen months and this city has given me moments that will live with me forever. I'm very proud and honoured to be the manager of York City. It really is a privilege.' The parade provided a fitting end to a season in which Mills had refused to put a ceiling on his side's potential achievements. His team were never beaten by more than a one-goal margin – another club record – while an average attendance of 3,097 at Bootham Crescent represented the highest figure during the Conference era.

Mills' men also overcame a fair amount of adversity to reach their goal. Prior to a ball being kicked in 2011/12, had any City supporter been told that the team would need to contend with long-term injuries to Walker, Kerr, McGurk and Oyebanjo over the next nine months, the perennial pre-season optimism might have been dampened somewhat. Had they also learned early in the campaign that Boucaud – such a fundamental figure in the team's swashbuckling start – would be sold to Luton in January, and Ingham would be replaced by Musselwhite in the three games left to clinch a play-off place, many would have been prone to panic.

But, not Mills, who likes his Guinness pints not half empty or even half full, he enjoys them with the creamy head spilling over the top. His players adopted that positivity and a long eight-year wait to hear eight wonderful words had ended – York City were back in the Football League.

Left: Jon Challinor grabs a first-round stoppage-time equaliser to keep York City in the 2012 FA Trophy. (Nigel Holland)

Below: Matty Blair heads in the goal at Luton that sends York to Wembley for the 2012 FA Trophy final. (Nigel Holland)

Ashley Chambers and Matty Blair in the back of the net following Exodus Geohaghon's own goal in the play-off semi-final first leg against Mansfield. (Nigel Holland)

Matty Blair gets another goal to send his team to Wembley, heading in at Field Mill to secure a 2-1 aggregate play-off semi-final win in extra-time. (Nigel Holland)

James Meredith celebrates with York fans at the end of the Mansfield match. (Nigel Holland)

The unstoppable Matty Blair gives York the lead against Newport in the FA Trophy final. (Nigel Holland)

Lanre Oyebanjo gets his team's second goal to secure a 2-0 FA Trophy final victory. (Nigel Holland)

Chris Smith lifts the FA Trophy. (Nigel Holland)

City players celebrate their Trophy triumph. (Nigel Holland)

York 'keeper Michael Ingham makes it third time lucky after two previous Wembley defeats. (Nigel Holland)

Lanre Oyebanjo, Jason McGill, Gary Mills and Matty Blair show off the FA Trophy on the banks of the River Ouse. (Anthony Chappel-Ross)

Ashley Chambers (left) wheels away after equalising against Luton in the Blue Square Bet Premier play-off final. (Nigel Holland)

Matty Blair (who else?) is the hero again after netting the winning goal to secure York City's place back in the Football League. (Nigel Holland)

Back in the Royal Box, Chris Smith lifts the Blue Square Bet Premier play-off final trophy. (Nigel Holland)

Right: The open-top bus winds through the streets of York, with thousands turning out to celebrate the club's historic double. (Frank Dwyer)

Below: Mills cannot disguise his delight. (Nigel Holland)

Jamie Reed, Paddy McLaughlin, Scott Kerr and Jason Walker get their hands on the FA Trophy. (Nigel Holland)

The banner says it all. (Nigel Holland)

9

'WE CAN DO SPECIAL THINGS HERE'

Gary Mills welcomed York City's first season back in the Football League in typical fashion – immediately signalling his intention to clinch back-to-back promotions for the only time in the club's history. Back then, few would have thought that the campaign would, in the final analysis, beg two questions – where did it go wrong for Mills and how did Nigel Worthington turn things around following his dismissal?

Despite losing free agents James Meredith and Adriano Moke to Bradford and Cambridge United respectively, the double-Wembley-winning manager was certainly not predicting a tough time for his team before the season kicked off. 'The target is the same again – promotion,' he insisted.

His on-pitch sentinel, skipper Chris Smith, was considerably more cautious when asked his thoughts on the challenge ahead. Having been a member of the club's last relegated side back in 2004, Smith reasoned, 'I think the standard is higher and you would be a fool to think otherwise. There are some big teams in the division, including those who have just been relegated from League One. But we are only concerned about bringing our form from last season into the new one and kicking on.'

Some of the seeds of Mills' downfall were perhaps sewn before a ball was even kicked in League Two. The contributions of his summer signings would, ultimately, fall way short of the levels required to strengthen the squad. Bootham Crescent old boys Jonathan Smith and Lee Bullock were both brought back to the club – the latter having left for Cardiff during the March of the ill-fated 2003/04 campaign. Oli Johnson and Danny Blanchett were recruited from Oxford and Burton respectively while out-of-contract winger Michael Coulson arrived from Grimsby and John McReady was bought from Darlington.

With the exception of Coulson and McReady, who both suffered long-term injuries, the rest of Mills' new faces would not see out the season at Bootham Crescent. Jonathan Smith (ten appearances), Blanchett (two), Bullock (two) and Johnson (one) started just fifteen games between them – the same amount as cruciate ligament victim Coulson – while McReady, who recovered from a broken collar bone in January, was still waiting to make his full debut by the end of the campaign having fallen completely out of favour under Mills' replacement Worthington. At least when Coulson was fit he did justify Mills' decision to bring him to the club, never more spectacularly than on the new season's opening day.

Doncaster – the town where relegation had been so painfully confirmed eight years earlier – provided a fitting venue for the Minstermen to announce their return to Football League action in a Capital One Cup first-round tie. The game was also a more closer affair than the last meeting with Coulson firing his new club in front from 25 yards against a Rovers team recently relegated from the Championship and destined to bounce straight back up. Bullock's second debut in a York shirt was less successful with his trip on David Cotterill leading to Doncaster's seventy-third-minute equaliser, scored from the penalty spot by Chris Brown, who had also played for the hosts back in 2004. After extra-time, the game was decided on penalties, which were controversially taken in front of the home fans under police advice. Coulson and Matty Blair subsequently lifted their spot-kicks over the bar and the Minstermen were knocked out.

An aggrieved Mills, who had ambitiously set his team the goal of reaching the tournament's final, said afterwards, 'The police decided that the penalties had to be taken at that end but that didn't make sense to me. I thought that would have been decided by a toss-up. I don't understand why the police have to get involved and, if that was going to be the case, we should have been told before kick-off because we worked hard to get through extra-time.'

The Minstermen's first game back in the Football League then ended in a 3-1 home defeat to Wycombe – the side's heaviest loss for eighteen months. In front of 4,591 fans – the biggest opening-day crowd at Bootham Crescent in nineteen years – goals from Matt Bloomfield, Sam Wood and Stuart Beavon saw the visitors swoop into a 3-0 lead after fifty-three minutes. Jason Walker replied with a goal every striker welcomes – the ball going in literally off his backside – but it was not enough to prompt the kind of comeback that typified the previous season.

A 'gutted' Mills remained positive at the final whistle, saying, 'I don't think they were any better than us. They scored with a deflection and a cracking goal in the first half.'

In the next game, Ashley Chambers' late goal helped the side gain their first point in a 2-2 draw at Morecambe, where Bootham Crescent old boy Richard Brodie had opened the scoring for the Shrimps. Back-to-back 3-1 wins were then racked up at Barnet and against Oxford on home soil before Blair became the first visiting player to find the net at Rotherham's impressive New York Stadium with the only goal in a Johnstone's Paint Trophy tie. It was also the Millers' first defeat at their new ground but, in mid-September, Burton became the first home team in England to beat Mills' men in almost a year.

Since a 3-2 defeat at Gateshead twelve months earlier, only Welsh pair Wrexham and Newport had defeated the travelling Minstermen. But a club record of four home games without scoring in a season was then equalled during a 4-0 Johnstone's Paint Trophy drubbing against Coventry with poor mistakes by experienced duo Clarke Carlisle and fit-again Scott Kerr contributing to the team's demise.

PFA chairman Carlisle had been brought in by Mills prior to the August transfer deadline after shelving his retirement plans. Former Scotland international Scott Dobie was also given a chance to prove himself after a year out of the game training to be a policeman but departed swiftly without making a single appearance. Amazingly, considering the struggle for potency at home, Mills' team had netted during twenty-three consecutive fixtures on the road – also a club record – with that run eventually coming to an end following a 0-0 draw at Southend.

City exited the FA Cup at the first-round stage, meanwhile, following a 4-3 extra-time replay thriller at AFC Wimbledon. Despite having Kerr sent off in the thirty-fifth minute, the visitors pushed the Wombles all the way with substitute Jamie Reed bagging a brace. That match, though, was one in a sequence of seven without a victory for Mills' side during a winless November with the poorest performance coming in a 3-0 home League defeat to Wimbledon that saw the hosts booed off the pitch.

Railing at growing critics of his 4-3-3 system afterwards, Mills argued, 'Why would I change a formation that has won us lots of games and got us promoted? I've never heard such rubbish if people want us to change because we've lost one game of football. Over the last twelve months, the system has seen us play entertaining football and made us hard to beat. I got boos because we lost one game. I'm glad I wasn't here when the team was losing every week before I was manager. It must have been horrendous.'

Carlisle, meanwhile, was offloaded to Northampton after news leaked of his intention to join the Sixfields club during the January transfer window. A disappointed Mills added, 'I brought somebody in who wasn't fixed up with a club but wanted to get back into the game. We gave him that opportunity and it took a number of games for him to get fit. His performances have been okay, maybe a bit mixed, but he's said he wants to go to Northampton and that's it. Football is what it is. We talk about loyalty in the game and sometimes you get it, but sometimes you don't.'

The last month of the year provided some cause for optimism, however, with transfer-listed midfielder Michael Potts bagging a brace on his first start of the season in a 3-2 success at Rochdale. Chambers went on to emulate him during a 4-1 home romp against Bristol Rovers – the club's biggest Football League win since 1995. But those results were intermingled with disappointing defeats at Plymouth (2-0) and Chesterfield (3-0) before the return of defensive stalwart David McGurk – just short of a year after his last appearance due to a combination of injury and Mills' reluctance to recall him – heralded a first clean sheet in eleven matches as 2012 ended with a 0-0 draw at Fleetwood.

Having bid farewell to one of the most cherished years in the club's history, 2013 then got off to a highly promising start when promotion contenders Burton were seen off 3-0 at Bootham Crescent thanks to Walker's penalty and further efforts from Paddy McLaughlin and Blair.

A pleased Mills said afterwards, 'Burton are a tough side to play against but we defended very well all over the park. We got three goals, a clean sheet and three points, so that's a fantastic start to the New Year.'

Hardly anybody would have forecast then that the game would represent Mills' last win in charge of the Minstermen and that he would be sacked just two months later. The team were six points short of the play-off positions at the time and twelve clear of the relegation zone. Off the pitch, meanwhile, it was announced that losses of £467,000 were made during the double-winning Wembley season, with 96 per cent of income having been spent on an estimated £1 million in playing costs, which included salaries, transfer fees and bonuses. Explaining the annual accounts results, the club's financial management consultant Peter Rookes said, 'This is the cost of promotion to the Football League. Throughout the club's time in the Conference, operating losses of this size were inevitable if York City wanted to put together a team that would compete and challenge for promotion. The accounts show that maximum resources were made available to Gary Mills to enable promotion to the Football League. Income from two successful Wembley trips totalling £235,000 ultimately helped keep the losses in line with the original budgets.'

Those figures meant the club had racked up approximately £2.22 million in operating losses during their eight seasons as a Conference outfit, highlighting how essential maintaining Football League status would be in the future with the consequent central funding allowing the Minstermen to operate on a break-even basis. But the unthinkable possibility that the club could become the first to go straight back down to the Conference since promotion was introduced in 1987 became a growing fear during an awful run of eleven games that would cost the previous season's messiah his job. Relegation would have almost certainly meant that owners JM Packaging would cease loaning money to the club, with no guarantee of a swift return to League Two. Part-time football at Bootham Crescent would also have been a likely prospect.

In between two highly-creditable draws with eventual champions Gillingham, alarm bells began to ring when Mills' side become the first Minstermen outfit since October 1981 to concede four goals in two consecutive League fixtures, going down 4-1 against Morecambe before losing 4-0 at Wycombe. Home 'keeper Jordan Archer was only called into action once in the latter match on eighty-nine minutes by loan signing Alex Rodman after Kerr and Jamal Fyfield had both conceded first-half penalties.

Mills called for unity at the club afterwards, saying, 'The game is not all about success and, when things aren't going right, you have to stand up and be counted. I have to do that as manager and the players need to do their jobs better. We know that and there's no hiding or excuses. We are going through a bad spell but you have to live with that. We've worked hard to get where we are and it's now a time to stick together – that's very important. I believe I have a dressing room of players that will work hard to get us out of this mess and I have to pick the right team. The last two results suggest that maybe I haven't. But players have to take responsibility because I rely on them for my job. I enjoy my job and I don't pick teams to lose games. It's a testing time and testing for me as manager, but I am going to come through it.'

Certain players Mills was relying on to keep his job were offering very little, however, especially those he had signed during an underwhelming transfer window in January. On-loan Blackburn defender Jack O'Connell was the one notable exception, but Icelandic premier division striker Ben Everson was swiftly packed off to Gateshead without making a start. Nor did Mills trust League of Ireland forward David McDaid enough to give him a full debut for the club, while Salford City defender Jameel Ible would later depart Bootham Crescent without even making the bench in a senior match. Subsequent loan signings Michael Rankine, returning to the club from Aldershot, Curtis Obeng and John McGrath also failed to reverse the flagging fortunes.

A 2-1 defeat against fellow strugglers Barnet, managed by former AC Milan and Holland legend Edgar Davids, represented the eighth game without a win and left Mills bristling at renewed criticism of his favoured formation. '4-3-3 has been very successful for us,' he claimed. 'The problem we have got is that we are giving goals away at this moment in time but, if the chairman wants a 4-4-2 manager, then I'm proud of what I have done at this club. People might be having a go at me and I'm having a hard time and finding things difficult, but we've got to stick together.'

The board responded with a statement from communications director Sophie Hicks that stopped short of the dreaded vote of confidence. She said, 'Clearly, for the club and everyone associated with it, including our supporters, we are expecting an improvement in results, starting on Saturday.'

Following a 0-0 draw with Oxford, the spoils were also shared at Rotherham where the home side snatched an ill-deserved point when Danny Nardiello pounced on ninety-four minutes after Rankine had failed to cut out a Ben Pringle cross, cancelling out Blair's second-half strike. The next game proved to be Mills' last with a 2-0 defeat to Capital One Cup finalists Bradford not only representing an eleventh game without victory but also leaving the club with just three wins from eighteen home matches and one goal from open play in nine encounters. Late goals by James Hanson and Garry Thompson heralded the end of Mills' two-and-a-half-year tenure. Emotional chairman Jason McGill subsequently explained the reasons for Mills' dismissal, while also paying tribute to the outgoing manager, saying, 'We must thank Gary Mills for what he did last season. He brought us out of the Conference and back into the Football League after eight years, so bringing him to the club was a very important decision that paid off. He made an unbelievable contribution because we did not have the biggest budget in the Conference. It wasn't the lowest, but it certainly wasn't the biggest. But everything conspired to go for us last season. We had a great team spirit and everything worked. Unfortunately, a record of six points from thirty-three in the Football League was difficult for us to accept as a board, but it's better to have fought and lost than not to have fought at all.'

Shedding light on how tough it had been for him to relieve Mills of his duties, McGill added, 'Decisions are easy to make but delivering them is very, very hard. The relationship we had with Gary was a very good one and I don't want anybody to be under the misconception that what we did after Saturday's game was anything other than very difficult, after what we achieved last season. But we have to think about the greater good of the football club and that's why the decision was made.'

In a poll, conducted by *The Press* at the time, 45 per cent of supporters were against Mills' dismissal, 41 per cent in favour and 14 per cent unsure. The manager departed, though, with his side having dropped to within four points of the relegation zone. In a frank post-match assessment of the Bradford game, less than an hour before his sacking, Mills said, 'There was nothing in the game but that's happened a few times this season. You have to score goals to win matches and we're not doing that. We had the better chances before they scored but, when you don't look like you can score goals, that escalates into a problem.'

Former Northern Ireland and Norwich manager Worthington was the man who inherited that problem when he was installed as the new manager two days later. Coaches Darron Gee, Des Lyttle and Paul Musselwhite, meanwhile, were, also relieved of their duties along with Mills as Worthington appointed former Walsall and Darlington goalkeeper Fred Barber as his assistant and promoted Steve Torpey from his head of youth football role to first-team coach. Extolling the merits of Mills' successor, McGill said, 'He knows people in the game and that will help in terms of player recruitment. We will be making sufficient funds available to assist him in that respect, as we have done with all our previous managers. His coaching ability cannot be questioned either. He has his UEFA Pro licence and has managed in the Premier League and at international level, so he comes with all that experience.'

On his decision to return to club management with the Minstermen after his international stint, Worthington explained, 'I've had a few offers from clubs in higher divisions during the last twelve months but they did not feel right for me. I spoke to the chairman here at great length though and there is a lot of common ground in our thoughts about how a football club should be run. I felt very comfortable with how realistic he is about how he wants the club to make steady and gradual progress. He doesn't want to put the club in jeopardy and, for me, that's the right way. I also know the history of the club and that it has been through some tough times over the last ten years. To fight back from where it has been was fantastic and now a lot of work has got to be done to move it forward again.'

The new manager immediately set a safety target of fifty points. His team were ten short of that tally with ten games left to play and Worthington admitted, 'I have to make an immediate impact because games are running out but there are ample points available to make sure we are in League Two next season.'

Skipper Smith scored twice in Worthington's first game as manager but could not save his side from another defeat to a relegation rival with the Minstermen going down 3-2 at AFC Wimbledon. As a consequence, Worthington became the first York manager since Viv Busby to start his reign with a defeat and went on to take just one point from a possible twelve in his first four games. During that period, the team drew 0-0 at home to Rochdale with McGrath managing the Minstermen's only shot on target in the ninetieth minute.

There were also demoralising defeats to promotion contenders Port Vale (2-0) and dogfight rivals Torquay, where on-loan Sheffield United striker and former England under-21 international Richard Cresswell marked his second debut for the club – fourteen years after leaving for Sheffield Wednesday in a £950,000 deal – with a consolation from the penalty spot in a 2-1 defeat.

While not quite *Mission Impossible* yet, even the intervention of Tom Cruise, Torquay's unimaginatively christened left-back, had not assisted the visitors in their battle to beat the drop. Cruise was sent off in the seventy-second minute following his shove on another Worthington loan signing Josh Carson, which led to Cresswell's 12-yard chance, but the visitors could not make their numerical advantage count during the remainder of the match. The result meant the Minstermen remained in the relegation zone they had tumbled into for the first time four days earlier when a 50:1 William Hill accumulator of unlikely results saw four of the teams previously below them in the standings all win their game in hand.

Commenting on the precarious situation, fit-again centre-back McGurk, who had played in all eight of the club's Conference campaigns, said, 'Relegation is not even worth thinking about. I've been here so long that I know how long it took to finally get out of the Conference and what promotion meant to everyone – the club, the fans and the chairman. We just can't let the club go back down. I've missed a lot of games in the last two years but everything boils down to a six-game season now.'

On Good Friday, though, the club even spent one night at the bottom of the League before a fairly nondescript 0-0 draw at Bristol Rovers – a club record-equalling ninth goalless stalemate of the season – proved to signal a turning point. In that game, on-loan Sunderland reserve Adam Reed and first-year professional Tom Platt, recalled from a loan spell with Harrogate Town, were paired in midfield to instil more energy into that area of the pitch with Dan Parslow moving into an anchoring role behind them. Lanre Oyebanjo, along with McGurk, had also returned to offer more solidity to the back four following injury.

The team then chose 1 April to belatedly make fools of anybody writing off their survival chances, halting a winless run that had become scarily reminiscent of the last time the club dropped out of the Football League.

Following three months and sixteen games without a victory, fellow strugglers Plymouth were seen off 2-0 at Bootham Crescent with Chambers and Cresswell the first-half marksmen. An opportunity to climb above

Accrington and out of the bottom two, however, was squandered in the next match when, agonisingly, Peter Murphy struck on ninety-three minutes to earn the visitors a point following Adam Reed's earlier strike. The scoreline represented a club record nineteenth draw of the season and, incredibly, the team would later finish the campaign with the same number of defeats (fifteen) as League Two runners-up Rotherham. Injuries to McGurk and Carson, however, added to the despair at the final whistle against Accrington.

The club were still in the relegation zone with three games left to play and promotion hopefuls Northampton, with ten consecutive home wins under their belt, were their next hosts. Worthington responded by handing teenager Tom Allan – a second-year scholar given professional terms by Mills earlier in the season – his first senior start in place of McGurk and recalled Blair following Carson's return to Ipswich. What came next was as remarkable as it was unexpected.

Following Chambers' seventh-minute strike, the Minstermen even contended with the first-half loss of attacking talisman Cresswell to a season-ending calf injury before wrapping up a first away triumph in twelve games courtesy of a John Johnson own goal, forced by Blair's lung-busting counter attack. The win also lifted the club three places out of the relegation zone they had occupied for four weeks.

Prior to his Bramall Lane return, Cresswell declared his pride at being a member of the side that had lifted his home-town club out of the bottom two and left willing the rest of the team to complete a successful fight against the drop. He said, 'I have been privileged to be part of that team over the last few weeks. It has been a fantastic turn around and, hopefully, I have played my part. Obviously, there is now a great platform there to go on and secure the club's League status and, hopefully, the lads will finish the job.'

Worthington, meanwhile, paid tribute to Cresswell's influence on and off the pitch during the club's resurrection, saying, 'He's been absolutely fantastic to have around the place over the last month. He's a great pro and a true York City fan and player through and through.'

Ahead of the penultimate match of the season and the final home fixture against Southend, communications director Hicks summed up the magnitude of the match, insisting, 'This game is just as important to the club as last season's play-off final at Wembley. We would like to encourage anyone with an interest in York City to come down to Bootham Crescent to show support for the team. Please give our players that extra boost to help them achieve another vital three points.'

The people of York answered the rallying cry with 5,975 – the biggest crowd of the season – turning up for a tense afternoon against a visiting side still harbouring play-off ambitions. With McGurk restored to the back four and Walker returning for Cresswell, goals from Adam Reed and Blair secured a 2-1 win but not before a couple of late scares. The visitors had an eighty-seventh-minue effort ruled out for offside and captain Smith cleared two chances off the line in stoppage time.

Incredibly, the result did not see Worthington's men safe, with a point still required on the final day of the season at Dagenham & Redbridge who, to add to the drama, needed a win to be sure of preserving their Football League status. Ahead of making his 300th appearance for the club in the crunch contest, club stalwart Parslow was fully focussed on the task in hand, saying, 'We've got dragged into this scrap and need to make sure we finish the job. We want to put to bed this tough, tough season because there's no getting away from it – that's what it has been. Hopefully, then, we can all look back and use it as a stepping stone to improve next season.'

Unbelievably, seven sides were still in danger going into the final programme of fixtures. But the scenario for York was pretty simple – if Wimbledon beat a Fleetwood team, with only pride to play for, at home and Barnet got at least a point at Northampton, who had already secured their play-off place and had no prospect of automatic promotion, then the Dagenham match would decide one of the two relegation spots.

An inevitably nervy first half was shaded by the hosts, who hit the post through Brian Woodhall. The same player went on to force Ingham into a fine save and lifted a further chance over the bar from

6 yards early in the second period. That miss, though, seemed to galvanise the visitors who made the breakthrough on sixty-seven minutes when skipper Smith, a colossus during Worthington's ten games in charge, turned and fired in his fourth goal of the season from 8 yards after Ingham's long free-kick into the penalty box had cannoned off Parslow's back.

Ingham would eventually celebrate his 106th clean sheet for the club – fourteen short of Happy Wanderer Tommy Forgan's all-time record – with a brilliant double save to deny Luke Howell and Woodhall at the death. Elsewhere, Wimbledon beat Fleetwood but Dagenham were saved by Barnet's 2-0 loss at Northampton, meaning the North London side went down with a record-high number of fifty-one points – one more than the target Worthington had set his side on taking the Bootham Crescent reins. It was an amazing end to a nerve-shredding campaign.

Following sixteen matches without a win, the team would have won their last five had it not been for Accrington's injury-time equaliser. On the season's finale in East London, Worthington said, 'It was a great day for the football club and a great achievement by the players. We have ended up staying up in style and the players have worked hard to get some excellent results. They have come on in leaps and bounds and it has been a real team and squad effort.' The manager also paid tribute to the team's loyal supporters, who drowned out any noise from their hosts. He added, 'I believe if you work together as a club, no matter what part of it you are, you can go a long way. It's been difficult for the supporters but they've backed us all the way through and they have got their just rewards. They really were our twelfth man at Dagenham and having nearly 1,200 there was phenomenal. I'm delighted for them and the directors and, hopefully, everyone can relax now, breathe easier and look forward.'

Among those moving on at the end of the season were Wembley heroes Blair, Walker, McLaughlin, Jamie Reed, Jon Challinor and Chris Doig, along with 2011/12 Supporters' and Players' Player of the Year Kerr, as Worthington swept the decks to usher in a new era at Bootham Crescent. There might not have been an open-top bus parade to mark the end of the club's first season back in the Football League but the 1,159 jubilant fans almost lifted the roof of Dagenham's away end as the final whistle signalled the end of 2012/13. That outpouring of relief was subsequently matched when Worthington announced he would be staying on as manager.

Dagenham goal hero and skipper Smith was certainly impressed by the impact made by the former Premier League boss, saying, 'He's been here ten games and I could not say a bad word about him. He had his way he wanted to play and it did not happen instantly but we took it on board gradually and he has a good pedigree to take this club forward.'

Smith and fellow loyal servants Ingham, McGurk and Parslow, along with the likes of Chambers, Oyebanjo and promising teenager Platt, should help in that respect in addition to a raft of summer signings.

With a new stadium on the horizon, meanwhile, Worthington turned his attentions to the future by predicting 'special things' at Bootham Crescent, saying, 'I am delighted to be York City's manager going forward. It is a club with great potential and I believe we can do special things here. I'm looking forward to the challenge ahead.' Smith and Worthington also had personal cause for celebration at the end of the campaign after winning League Two's respective Player and Manager of the Month awards. Those accolades convinced chairman Jason McGill, who had been involved throughout the fight back from the dark days of administration and relegation from the Football League, that the club was now in safe hands heading into 2013/14.

'We were only interested in one person taking this club forward and that was Nigel Worthington,' he insisted. 'During our last ten games of the [2012/13] season, he displayed exceptional managerial skills and impressed us with his work ethic and total professionalism. We are very pleased to have a manager in place who can help us improve the club and build for a better future.'

It was a sentiment most would have echoed at Bootham Crescent. After almost a decade of fighting back, everybody involved with the club was now ready to look forward.

They all count! York City's first goal back in the Football League goes in off Jason Walker's backside, with Jonathan Smith watching on. It cannot prevent a 3-1 defeat to Wycombe though. (Gary Atkinson)

Above: David McGurk receives a memento for reaching 300 appearances for the club from Gary Mills. (Michael Tipping)

Right: Michael Coulson celebrates scoring during the first home win back in the Football League – a 3-1 triumph over old adversaries Oxford. (Mike Tipping)

Left: Nigel Worthington begins the stiff task of keeping York City in the Football League. (Anthony Chappel-Ross)

Below: Returning hero Richard Cresswell gets the second goal in a 2-0 win over Plymouth – the club's first victory in seventeen matches. (Garry Atkinson)

Adam Reed (left) celebrates his crucial goal at Southend with teammate Ashley Chambers. (Michael Tipping)

Nigel Worthington and Chris Smith show off their League Two Manager and Player of the Month awards. (Garry Atkinson)

APPENDICES

2012/13 Football League Appearances

Chris Smith	50	Alex Rodman	18	Adam Reed	6
Matty Blair	49	Chris Doig	16	Tom Allan	5
Jason Walker	48	Clarke Carlisle	14	Josh Carson	5
Ashley Chambers	42	Michael Potts	14	Richard Cresswell	5
Jamal Fyfield	37	Jonathan Smith	14	Charlie Taylor	5
Paddy McLaughlin	33	Lee Bullock	13	Danny Blanchett	4
Lanre Oyebanjo	32	Danny Kearns	12	David McDaid	4
Scott Kerr	31	David McGurk	11	John McReady	4
Jon Challinor	22	John McGrath	9	Curtis Obeng	4
Michael Coulson	21	Michael Rankine	8	Ben Everson	2
Jamie Reed	19	Oli Johnson	7		
Jack O'Connell	18	Tom Platt	7		

2012/13 Football League Goals

Ashley Chambers	10	Paddy McLaughlin	4	Richard Cresswell	2
Jason Walker	9	Jamie Reed	4	Adam Reed	2
Matty Blair	7	Chris Smith	4	Dan Parslow	1
Michael Coulson	5	Michael Potts	3	Alex Rodman	1

York City Top Ten Players' Appearances in Conference, FA Trophy, FA Cup and Conference Shield (2004–12)

David McGurk	296	James Meredith	163	Michael Rankine	104
Daniel Parslow	250	Ben Purkiss	149	Martyn Woolford	102
Michael Ingham	214	Manny Panther	136		
Richard Brodie	164	Craig Farrell	111		

York City Top Ten Players' Goals Scored in Conference, FA Trophy, FA Cup and Conference Shield (2004–12)

Richard Brodie	72	Craig Farrell	24	Matty Blair	20
Clayton Donaldson	44	Michael Rankine	24	Jason Walker	18
Andy Bishop	37	Onome Sodje	24		
Martyn Woolford	25	Jamie Reed	21		